GOD'S WORD
In Man's Language

GOD'S WORD
In Man's Language

by Eugene A. Nida

HARPER & BROTHERS
PUBLISHERS, NEW YORK

Library of Congress catalog card number: 52-5466

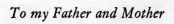

To my Father and Mother

CONTENTS

CONTENTS

PREFACE

Working with Bible translators in many of the remote regions of the world has provided a unique opportunity to study some of the fascinating phases of translating the Scriptures into hundreds of languages. On our trips, which have taken us to more than thirty countries and have introduced us to some of the problems in more than eighty languages, my wife and I have made extensive notes on the technical and human-interest features of this dramatic task in which missionaries work out alphabets, grammars, and dictionaries of strange languages and then use these language tools to proclaim the message of God's Word. In the preparation of this book we have sought to share with others the spiritual thrills which have been ours as we have seen the unfolding of this strategic part of the missionary's ministry.

We wish to express our sincere appreciation to the many missionaries who have provided the numerous illustrations presented in these pages. These persons are in many instances almost unknown except to their own immediate associates and to the native peoples who are so indebted to them for what they have done in laying the foundation for effective evangelization by providing God's Word in their languages.

This volume is designed not only for the pastor and Sunday-school teacher, who may wish to find illustrative material for sermons and lessons, but also for the layman who desires some introduction into a previously unexplored realm of Christian experience.

For the aid of the reader there are three indexes: (1) a Scriptural Index, which lists in Biblical order the passages which are mentioned in the book, (2) a Language Index, which also includes the geographical location of little-known languages, and (3) a General Index, which lists the topics and Scriptural expressions.

American Bible Society
New York, 1951   EUGENE A. NIDA

GOD'S WORD
In Man's Language

CHAPTER 1

EVERY MAN IN HIS OWN LANGUAGE

"But how do you say 'God redeemed us' so that your own Bambara people can understand?" the missionary inquired earnestly, as he endeavored to find out from his West African translation helper how to express in the Bambara language the meaning of "redeem"— that key word of the Scriptures.

"Why—we say 'God took our heads out,'" was the strange reply.

"But how will the people understand that?"

"Oh, that is easy. Perhaps you forget, but tales of the Arab slave raids into the interior live vividly in the memories of our fathers." And then this Bambara man continued to explain about the long lines of lash-driven men and women wearily walking to the coast, each with a heavy iron collar around his neck and with a chain leading from one slave to another. It so happened that at times in the villages through which these lines of condemned slaves passed, a local chief or king might see some friend being led away to slavery, and he would want to redeem him. This he could do if he paid the Arabs enough gold, silver, brass, or ivory. To redeem a friend he would literally "take his head out of the iron collar." *bought -- freed*

And so today Bambara evangelists, as they tell the people of God's redeeming love in Christ Jesus, explain to the huddled bands around the evening village fire that God saw us in slavery to sin and self, being driven under the lash of Satan, and so He sent His Son to die that men might live. Thus He redeemed us, literally, "He took our

13

heads out." "And furthermore," they explain, "just as in ancient times a redeemed slave felt an obligation to serve for a lifetime the one who had thus redeemed him, so we may be the voluntary slaves of Jesus Christ." *bondslaves- Paul, Rom 1*

This expression "to redeem," literally, "to take the head out," was born of the bitter experience of slavery, but it has come to be the very vehicle of thought by which men may know the truth of God, who alone can set them free. *Man's suffering provides the language for the love + atonement of God.*

Already the Bible or some portions of it have been translated into and published in 1,034 languages. The entire Bible exists in 191, and the New Testament in 246 others, while current publications of Scripture exist in some 650 languages.[1] However, there are at least 1,000 more languages and dialects in the world which have absolutely nothing of the Word of God. Of course, the speakers of these 1,000 languages do not represent large tribes and nations, but their total population is fully equal to that of the United States.

To meet the needs of the 1,000 groups without the Scriptures and to provide the Word of God more adequately for those who already have some of it, there are today more missionaries engaged in Bible translating and revision than at any other time in the history of the world. This work may not seem as exciting as trekking through animal haunts and braving formidable jungles, or as thrilling as preaching to those who have never heard the Story, or as rewarding as ministering to the daily needs of mind and body; and yet the journey into the secret realms of a people's language introduces one to the soul of a nation and makes it possible to lay the foundation for teaching the Truth as it is found in the revelation of God to men through the Scriptures. Relatively fewer missionaries have undertaken the thankless task of exploring queer sounds, strange

[1] The translations which are not included in this figure of 650 fall into three principal classes: (1) dead languages, e.g., Syriac, Gothic, and Massachusetts, (2) those which were produced as linguistic or literary exhibits, e.g., numerous translations of the Songs of Solomon in various European dialects, under the sponsorship of Prince Louis Lucien Bonaparte, a nephew of the Emperor Napoleon, and (3) those which have been of very limited use or circulation because of inferior quality or lack of adequate continuing missionary work.

words, and even stranger meanings, but those who have made this journey have a marvelous story to tell.

These missionary pioneers have rarely found a dictionary or grammar of the language which they determined to learn. In fact, in many instances there is not so much as an alphabet. One must simply sit down with natives and begin to ask for words—sometimes without so much as being able to say, "What do you call this?" It may take weeks to stumble across this key phrase. At first, one may be forced to sit and stick out one's lower lip and in this way point to objects, for there are several places in the world where pointing with the finger is a very crude, vulgar gesture.

Sounds may give no end of trouble. The natives seem to understand one another perfectly, but the queer things that come out as sounds to be symbolized by an alphabet seem like so many squeals, squeaks, grunts, pops, and hisses, with queer vowels added at the most difficult places. Some languages have clicklike sounds, where the air pops into the mouth before the following vowel comes out. Almost anyone can say Tsk! Tsk! (in admonishing children) or suck in the air along the sides of the mouth as when driving horses, but in the Bushman and Hottentot languages of South Africa there are twenty different types of these clicks, and all of them become a regular part of the word-making genius of the language. It is hard enough for many missionaries to distinguish between such simple pairs as the two Conob[2] words *tsu* "spit" and *ts'u* "kiss." What we write as *ts'* in the second word stands for a kind of explosive sound, which may be described as a sort of "spitting." But why this sound should be associated with the word meaning "kiss" and not the word meaning "spit," where it seems so logically to belong, is more than anyone can explain. It is just one of those strange anomalies which occur in languages everywhere.

If sounds were the only trouble, then it would be relatively easy, but some languages have grammars which almost defy description.

[2] A Mayan language spoken in Guatemala.

at least for the beginner. Imagine running into a Bolivian Quechua word like this:

$$ruwanayashaskasniyquichejmantaka$$

Thirty-two letters is not too bad; but when one finds that this word is made up of eight distinct grammatical parts and that the parts must always occur in just this order and that the entire word means "concerning your continually accomplishing your future work"—well, it is enough to stump some of the experts. In the Quechua language of Bolivia it is possible to take almost any verb root and add more than 50,000 combinations of at least twenty different sets of suffixes and particles which combine to make up these complicated forms.

Some missionaries who have been undaunted in the face of strange and complicated grammars of so-called primitive languages have thought they might have clearer sailing when they came to learning the vocabulary of such "culturally inferior" peoples. But imagine their surprise to find in a language such as Zulu 120 different words to describe distinct kinds of walking—walking pompously, with a swagger, crouched, in tight clothes—to cite only a few. Or consider the consternation of the missionaries in Madagascar who found that the Malagasy-speaking native distinguishes more than 200 different kinds of noises and has special words and phrases to differentiate over 100 different colors.

With all the welter of strange sounds, queer grammatical forms, and myriads of new words, is it any wonder that one poor missionary in Central Africa was so confused that he told the people, "Go sit on a stick," rather than "Enter the kingdom of heaven"? Another missionary in Congo was always talking about John the Baptist "crying" in the wilderness and the prophets of old "crying" out to the people. But his literal translation applied only to the crying of little babies before they were old enough to talk. How utterly incomprehensible his message must have been—for all of God's messengers seemed to be squalling children.

Literal translations—the easiest and the most dangerous—are the source of many mistakes. The missionary in Latin America who constantly used the phrase "it came to pass" scarcely realized that it only meant to the people, "something came in order to pass there." The phrase was just one more meaningless confusion in the midst of an already difficult context. In one language of West Africa the missionaries had translated literally the story of Mary "sitting at the feet of Jesus," only to discover later that what they had said really described Mary as "on Jesus' lap."

It is one thing to speak of "heaping coals of fire on one's head" if one is talking to an English-speaking congregation; but if one speaks that way in some parts of Africa, he can be badly misunderstood, for that is one method of torture and killing.

Perhaps the gravest errors have come because a well-intentioned translator has simply taken a native's word for the meaning. But he will soon discover that he must check and double-check every word and phrase. Only after some time was it discovered that in one language of Liberia the natives were reciting a portion of the Lord's Prayer as "Do not catch us when we sin" rather than "Lead us not into temptation." Because of very inadequate knowledge of the native idiom, early missionaries had not been able to explain the Lord's Prayer—certainly not this phrase—and so the natives simply inserted what would make sense to them. To so many peoples of earth—primitive and "civilized"—sin is not sin unless one is caught. These Liberian natives were only a little more frank about their beliefs and were appropriating a little Scriptural sanction for them.

The mistakes in some translations are not so easily discovered, for they require a very profound knowledge of the peoples and their customs. For example, in the Aztec dialect of Zacapoaxtla in Mexico it is impossible to translate literally the phrase of John 8:56, "Your father Abraham rejoiced to see my day." This statement, as made by Jesus, would have meant to the Aztecs of that region that Jesus was actually an animal, living in incestuous sin, but disguised as a medicine man, for they believe that a medicine man is really not a

Jake.

human, but an evil animal. However, during the day this creature puts on the guise of a man and calls his false appearance "my day."

Even those usages hallowed by time must not go unchallenged. In one language of East Africa missionaries have been saying for more than fifty years, "The Lord be with thy spirit," but they never realized until recently that because of subtle grammatical distinctions this important benediction actually implied, "Yes, the Lord be with *your* spirit, for we don't want him." When this fact was discovered, the missionaries protested to their native brethren and demanded why they would permit missionaries to go on making such a mistake for so many years. The only reply from the natives was that the missionaries were in the habit of saying a good many strange things, and since the missionaries all agreed in making the mistake, it must have been true, regardless of the strange implications. But this is scarcely less incongruous than the manner in which we have taken the Mizpah declaration, "The Lord watch between me and thee while we are absent one from the other," and have twisted it from its original context in which two jealous, cheating men called upon God for protection one from the other, and have appropriated it as a request for mutual blessings and benefits.

The journey into the soul of a language is often confusing because our idioms, which are the signposts of our thoughts, seem to have no counterparts, or at least no ready equivalents. In fact, the correspondence often appears to be quite contradictory. For example, those long, lanky Shilluk natives of the Anglo-Egyptian Sudan speak of a stingy man as "having a big heart" and a generous man as "having a small heart." This seems ridiculous to us, but not to Shilluk natives, who are every bit as well prepared to defend their idiom, as we are ours. They argue that a stingy, selfish man is one who has grabbed everything he can and has stored it away in his heart. Therefore, his heart is large. However, the generous man is one who has given away practically all that he has, and therefore his heart is small. This makes perfectly good sense and is fully as adequate as our corresponding idioms. But in the strangeness of such idiomatic metaphors we often become confused, and instead of blaming ourselves we are likely to insist that the natives are the ignoramuses, rather than ourselves. When the Mazatec people of Mexico speak of miracles as "long-necked things," one might think that this is no way to talk about the supernatural acts of Christ, but with a little more scrutiny this expression becomes a vivid picture-word. Supernatural events are the very things which make people stretch their necks to see what has happened. Here is a vivid characterization of the curious multitude who constantly followed Jesus.

The Valiente Indians of Panama talk of people in authority, but they have no abstract word for authority—rather, a short and simple phrase, "those on the handle." This does not mean a thing to us, but the Valientes grasp the significance of Mark 11:28 ("By what authority do you do these things?") literally, "What people on the handle told you to do these things?" The Valientes regard the ruler as the one who has the handle of the hunting knife in his hand. That is to say, "He is on the handle," while others could only grasp the blade, and of course would be injured in doing so. Hence, only the ruler can wield the knife and control its power; it is he who has the authority.

With all these rich figures of speech some people still question whether the so-called primitive languages have sufficient word resources to express spiritual and Biblical concepts. Such a judgment often represents a self-gratifying mixture of egotism and ignorance, but it must be thoroughly refuted. Of course, one will not find during the first few days of language exploring those rich words of spiritual truth such as "love," "faith," "joy," "grace," and "salvation." In fact, satisfactory terms may elude the searching missionary-translator for weeks and months. Just as the prospector does not discover diamonds and gold at the first glance, neither does the hunter for words find the gems of the language during the first days of patient inquiry. But that does not mean that the people have no proper terms for spiritual truths. A Valiente can talk of "hope in God," but he says quite picturesquely "resting the mind in God."

The phrase "resting the mind" implies waiting and confidence, and what is a better definition of hope than "confident waiting"? What we might define prosaically, the Valiente can picture in unforgettable figures of speech.

In some instances these spiritual terms result from adaptations reflecting the native life and culture. Among the Gbeapo people of Liberia a missionary wanted some adequate term for "prophet," and she was fully aware that the native word for "soothsayer" or "diviner" was no equivalent for the Biblical prophet who spoke forth for God. Of course, much of what the prophets said referred to the future, and though this was an essential part of much of their ministry, it was by no means all. The right word for the Gbeapo people would have to include something which would not only mean the foretelling of important events but the proclamation of truth as God's representative among the people. At last the right word came; it was "God's town-crier." Every morning and evening the official representative of the chief goes through the village crying out the news, delivering the orders of the chief, and announcing important coming events. "God's town-crier" would be the official representative of God, announcing to the people God's doings, His commands, and His pronouncements for their salvation and well-being. For the Gbeapo people the prophet is no weird person from forgotten times; he is as real as the human, moving message of the plowman Amos, who became God's town-crier to a calloused people.

As the heedless traveler sometimes overlooks an object of priceless value because he does not recognize its worth, so the translator may be tempted to discard as useless some rare phrase, which so skillfully disguises its fuller meaning in the rich secrets of native life. This was precisely the experience of Miss Estella Myers, a missionary working among the Karré people of French Equatorial Africa. She had tried so hard to explain to native helpers the meaning of the "Comforter." This term, transliterated as the *Paraclete* from Greek, is one of the most difficult in the Bible to render adequately. In order to find something fitting, she had explained at great length the ministry and work of the Holy Spirit as he encourages, exhorts, admonishes, protects, comforts, and guides the Christian. Finally, her native assistants exclaimed, "Oh, if anyone would do all of that for us, we would say, 'He's the one who falls down beside us.'" This seemed to be a completely inadequate, unfit phrase to describe the work of the Holy Spirit, and it would have soon been rejected had not the native brethren insisted on explaining the very special way in which this word is used.

When porters, carrying heavy loads on their heads, go on long journeys, often for as long as two or three months, they may become sick with malaria or dysentery, and in their weakness they straggle to the end of the line of carriers. Finally in complete exhaustion they may collapse along the trail, knowing full well that if they do not get to the safety of the next village, they will be killed and eaten by wild animals during the night. If, however, someone passing along the trail sees them lying there prostrate, and if he takes pity on them, stooping down to pick them up and helping them to reach the safety and protection of the next village, they speak of such a person as "the one who falls down beside us." It is this expression which the missionary translator has taken to translate "Comforter," for this is the One who sustains, protects, and keeps the children of God on their journey toward their heavenly home.

There is no lack of words and phrases to express spiritual truths once the missionary has learned intimately the life of the people. However, even in an apparent inadequacy there may be rich spiritual significance. For example, in the Cuicatec and Tzeltal languages of Mexico there is no way of distinguishing between "to believe" and "to obey." At first glance the absence of such a distinction would seem to point to the inadequacy of a language, and yet in this very lack of a distinction there is a truth which challenges our own thinking. These Indians of Mexico, who are regarded by so many as unutterably backward and uncultured, are quite frankly surprised by the distinction which we insist on making between "to believe" and "to obey." They reason—and rightly so—that these words should be one. "But if you believe, do not you obey?" they say. "And if you obey, does that not show that you believe?" Their contention is perfectly valid. It is we who are at fault. We make distinctions where no distinction should be made, and by the very abundance of our vocabulary we deceive ourselves into a subtle kind of hypocrisy which permits us to imagine that we are believers in God when we continue to disobey Him. The sensible person will admit that these Cuicatec and Tzeltal Indians, for all their apparent backwardness, are closer to the truth than we are. At least, they are not so prone to engage in the religious schizophrenia which badly divides personalities in our more "civilized" world and permits us to count ourselves as "believers" when in reality we are only deceiving ourselves—certainly not our neighbors.

We must not imagine that all missionary translators learn unwritten languages. Many translators go to areas where they must master languages with long literary heritages. Most missionaries to India, Burma, Siam, China, and Japan are not required to make up alphabets and grammars—though sometimes the ones in use are so unnecessarily complicated that it would be almost as well if one could start from scratch. But these languages also present their problems. The most obvious one is the intricacy of the orthography. The alphabet may be one derived from ancient Sanskrit and may represent more or less accurately the sounds of the language, or there may be no alphabet at all—just pictographic writing, with each word symbolized by a separate character, as in Chinese. Or there may be a combination of such symbols with syllabic writing added, as in the system which has constituted the traditional method of writing Japanese.

Nevertheless, as bad as such systems of writing may be, they are not as complicated as the vocabularies and the dialect distinctions which exist vertically even within the same language. We say "vertically," for these are not dialects which mark various regions of the country, but dialects which mark people. They are more difficult to overcome, for they represent man-made systems, sometimes designed for exploitation or caste preservation. What is one to do in a language where the religious vocabulary is borrowed almost entirely from Pali, a derivative of ancient Sanskrit and the language of the Buddhist priesthood? Such words are sanctioned through time and usage by those regarded as the religious leaders, but these words are often almost as meaningless to the common people as the Latin mass is to many English-speaking people. The words may "smell of holiness," but they do not instruct men in holiness.

So strong has been the hold of literary tongues and religious vocabularies upon the people of the Orient that only very slowly has this chain of tradition been broken here and there. But as men clamor for the truth and seek to know the revelation of God for themselves, they are not content with fine-sounding words; they want plain, meaningful words. For this reason in 1950 the revision committee for the Japanese Bible halted its work in the very middle of its extensive program of Scripture revision in order to start again—this time to translate into the language of the man in the street.

Putting eternal truths into the speech of everyday life reflects exactly the style of the Greek New Testament. The New Testament books were not written in the high-flown Asian style of the school-masters of the first and second centuries A.D.; they were couched in the words of the common people, who were seeking the truth about the living, risen Christ. For those who sought life, the dead forms of outmoded grammatical styles were useless. So today, the mission-ary translator carries on that same tradition, giving people the Word of God in their own living language, though the idioms may seem strange to us. For example, the Uduks along the Ethiopian border speak of "worry" and "being troubled" as "shivering in one's liver." John 14:1 does not sound like English: "Do not shiver in your livers; you believe in God, believe also in me." But the Scrip-tures in Uduk are not being translated for us, but for Uduks who must understand the meaning of the gospel in terms of their lives, not ours. The Navajos speak of "worry," but quite differently. They say, "My mind is killing me." Perhaps these Navajos are better psychologists than we had suspected. Only now do we begin to understand some of the deadly results of psychosomatic ailments. Worry can in the end be just as deadly as any other kind of disease, and the Navajos have sensed this truth. We are not to suppose that Navajos arrived at this expression by any long and involved scientific examination and investigation of worrying, but in their folkway idiom they have unconsciously recognized what we pay psychiatrists to tell us.

There are some people who see in the unusual idioms of primitive languages certain expressions which seem repulsive and quite below the dignity of religious experience. This has been true of the word which the Cuicatec Indians of Mexico have used for "worship." It contains the same root as for a dog wagging his tail. The only difference is that the pronoun subject, included in the verb, indicates that it refers not to an animal, but to a human. One could define the Cuicatec word as meaning literally "to wag the tail before God," that is, "to worship God." Some people would insist that such a word is unbecoming to the religious life and tends to make animals of men, thus lowering the dignity of human personality. Nothing of the kind! These Cuicatec Indians have simply recognized that in true worship there is something very much akin to the behavior of a dog toward his master. It would be well indeed if people were as devoted and genuine in their recognition of God as a dog is of his master. What dog denies his master, even in the courtroom when serious judgment is involved? And yet there is many a person who denies his Lord when the pressure of circumstances makes it the "socially approved" thing to do. These Cuicatec Indians, in their failure to distinguish between "believe" and "obey"[3] and in this relating of "worship" to the attitude of a dog toward his master, have exhibited keener insight than many a religious philosopher, whose theories dangle from abstract beams, suspended by the sky-

[3] See p. 21.

hooks of his own theories of religious evolution. Words for the religious life must be rooted in the daily experience of people for whom the religious life *is* life, and not just a theory about some neatly isolated part of life.

On the other hand, we must not get the impression that so-called primitive peoples have some intuitive perception which civilization has utterly destroyed. All peoples describe certain aspects of life in clumsy, awkward phrases, while employing vivid word pictures to symbolize other types of experience. The Kikwango name for "alms," literally "gifts of love," is one of these vivid expressions. Certainly alms should be "gifts of love," and not just the response from the motive of civic pride in wearing a red feather during the local community chest drive. Similarly, when the Barrow Eskimos call a "hymn" a "song of prayer," they have captured very graphically the real meaning of sacred music.

Despite the fact that many Christians recognize in a general way the importance of the Bible in the life of the Church, they seem to regard its translation into primitive tongues as more or less a waste of time. "Just tell them the story, and go on!" one hears so often. But these people have never dreamed of the distortions which may creep into a story which is only repeated by word of mouth. One missionary in Congo began to check up on some of the explanations of his Bibleless believers, and he found some amazing things: The name of Jairus' daughter was Zacchaeus, according to one man, and the poor man who was let down through the roof was said by another to be suffering from yaws; poor Bartimaeus was described as suffering from one blind eye, malaria, and leprosy; the foolish virgins forgot to bring their hearts—not their oil flasks; and one of the people in the temple who rejoiced to see the infant Jesus was said to have been King David himself. Such complete confusion seems incredible, but no more strange than would be the explanations of spiritual truths presented by English-speaking persons whose total Christian teaching consisted of a few weeks of Sunday school instruction, given by teachers, who in turn had only heard the stories of the Bible, and had not read or studied them for themselves.

Some persons are convinced that native peoples should have the Scriptures, but they seem to see no good reason at all for giving all four Gospels. Some even question the providence of God and the historical decisions of the Church in preserving these four accounts, of which three—Matthew, Mark, and Luke—are so similar. The missionary translator, however, has reason to see in practical experience the value of these different depictions of our Lord. For the Mohammedan world the popular Gospel is Matthew, for there in the first verse is Abraham; and there follows immediately a genealogy, which gives Jesus the distinction and importance that such a person should have, as far as Mohammedans are concerned. For the semi-Christianized person of Roman Catholic background, who has often heard much more about Mary than about the Son of God, the book of Luke is an introduction which leads from true reverence for Mary to the worship of Him who redeemed mankind and stands as the only mediator between God and man. For the philosophical Hindu or Buddhist the Gospel of John frequently strikes fire, for here is a point of contact, and the Word of God begins to live. For the native of most aboriginal societies, the best book is Mark, which has no difficult genealogy (as do Matthew and Luke), no series of Old Testament allusions (as in the beginning of Luke), and no philosophic declarations (as "In the beginning was the Word"). Here in Mark is the story of a man who was baptized, recognized by God, and then submitted to temptation—a story which moves quickly into the realm of all men's understanding.

The Bible translator may begin with any one of the Gospels, but he soon finds that one is not enough. There must be another, and another. Furthermore, the growing church must have the story of the Acts of the Apostles, for this is the story of the first-century church. Nor must doctrine be overlooked, and soon he is busy with Romans, I Corinthians, Galatians, etc., but these are scarcely completed when he senses a need among the native brethren for the heart-warming passages of the pastoral Epistles, for the hope of Revelation, for the story of beginnings in Genesis, for the spiritual grandeur of the Psalms, for the message of a coming Messiah in Isaiah, and for the story of suffering Job. The growth of the church and the training of its leadership demands the translation of the whole counsel of God, and with this must come commentaries and study books that men may read and understand more fully.

The true Bible translator follows closely in the tradition of Philip and Andrew, who led the inquiring Greeks to the Master in response to their request, "We would see Jesus." Presenting Jesus by the written Word, that by the Spirit of God men may have faith in the Living Word, is the goal and purpose of all translating. The greatest reward that any translator can receive is the one expressed by a Mazatec Indian woman in southern Mexico, who exclaimed as she read the Gospel of Mark, "Oh, it is just as though I could see Jesus."

That's how the written word corresponds with the living Christ,

CHAPTER 2

QUEER SOUNDS,
STRANGE
GRAMMARS, AND
RARE WORDS

The only thing worse than having to learn the alphabet of a language like Siamese, with its tiny circles, queer hooks, and intricate combining of letters, or one like Amharic, with its angular vowel prongs sticking out from awkwardly shaped consonants, is being required to work out an alphabet, beginning with nothing but a maze of unfamiliar sounds. If a missionary has had some preliminary training in phonetics or language structure, the task is so much easier,[1] but more often than not one arrives in some out-of-the-way spot with little or no linguistic preparation, and the words of the strange aboriginal tongue seem to flood into one's ears like so much meaningless jinglejangle. "The people talk so incessantly fast!" more than one missionary has exclaimed. In fact, that is precisely the reaction which everyone has to any foreign language. Strange sounds of unknown words always seem terribly fast.

But the speed with which natives seem to speak is not the only distracting matter; some of the sounds are exasperatingly complicated,

[1] See *Learning a Foreign Language* by Eugene A. Nida, a book published especially for the help of missionaries by the Division of Foreign Missions of the National Council of the Churches of Christ.

28

and the process of mastering them is tortuously difficult. One wide-spread difficulty in Africa is the pronunciation of double consonants. The sounds written as *gb* and *kp* do not consist of sequences of *g* and then *b* or of *k* and then *p*. Rather, the combinations *gb* and *kp* are pronounced simultaneously. Try pronouncing, if you will, the word *Ngbaka,* the name of an African language. This does not contain a sequence of *n, g,* and *b,* each with neat, clear-cut divisions. The *n*-sound begins with the tongue humped up in the back of the mouth, and the air going out of one's nose, but this lasts only for an instant, for immediately after this the lips close, the air through the nose is shut off, and then *g* and *b* are pronounced at the same time.

Some people do not have too much trouble with trilling their uvula—we all do it when we snore and can learn to do it when we gargle—but trilling the tip of the tongue is a little harder. In fact, in trying to make their tongues flipflop back and forth some people exert so much effort that the tongue becomes as stiff as a pump handle. The resulting noise is just a bad rumble. But imagine having to trill your lips! That is just what many missionaries must learn to do. For example, in the Yipounou language of the Gabon, in French Equatorial Africa, the word for an "odor" is *mbbunga.* The word begins with a queer kind of *m,* and then the sound written as two *b*'s is simply a trill of the two lips—pronounced more or less as a person would exclaim about the cold.

There are hosts of queer sounds in even queerer languages—queer, that is, only to us, for the sounds we make are equally strange and nonsensical to others. How unwieldy become our combinations of consonants when we say something like *glimpsed streams!* Between the vowel *i* of the first word and the vowel of the second there are seven different consonant sounds; in our writing we break them up by an *e,* but we do not pronounce the vowel. The Ngbakas of northern Congo think it strange that we should put our lower lip against our upper teeth when we pronounce an *f* or a *v.* It seems so much more sensible to them to put their lower lip inside of the upper teeth, and then to let it pop out as in the *b*-sound of *kakaba* "crow."

The task of mastering a language is not so difficult if there is someone in the tribe who speaks some foreign language which the missionary also knows; but if there is not as much as a single word in common, the initial stages may seem agonizingly difficult. When Efrain Alphonse first went to live and work among the Valiente Indians of Panama, he did not know a word of their language, and they knew nothing of his. At first he tried to find someone who knew some pidgin Spanish or English, learned from the sailors who skirted the coast in their small boats, purchasing coconuts and bananas from the natives in exchange for bright cloth and gaudy jewelry. But there was no one who could help him learn how to use the language. One small boy, with a big contagious grin and a willingness to be helpful to the new schoolteacher (for Mr. Alphonse had come to begin a mission school for these Valiente people), came bringing a gourd of fresh water from the spring, and immediately Mr. Alphonse tried to elicit his name by gesticulations and pidgin Spanish. The little fellow replied, "Tikonyaka"; and from then on Mr. Alphonse would call out, "Tikonyaka!" when he wanted the boy to come, but soon he discovered that the people were laughing and also calling him "Tikonyaka." It was only later that he discovered the real meaning of *tikonyaka*. It was actually a phrase meaning "I have no name." Often among the Valientes a small child does not have a personal name, but is known as the child of such and such a man or woman. The bright little fellow had properly interpreted Mr. Alphonse's question and had answered it as best he could. Without some common language, however, only a trial-and-error method of probing the meanings and uses of words can reveal the intricate and strange structures.

Strange vowels and consonants are one bad headache—as well as a tongue and jaw ache—especially when, as in Dinka (a Nilotic language of the Sudan) there are fourteen primary and secondary vowel qualities, all of which are long or short, giving twenty-eight;

and all of these are breathy or nonbreathy,[2] giving fifty-six. But this is not all of the trouble; there are differences of tone which distinguish between words. For example, *iän chi kwin cham* with *chi* pronounced on a mid tone means "I am not going to eat food," but the same phrase with a *chi* occurring on a high tone means, "I ate food."[3]

These differences of tones, called inflections of the voice by some people, are the source of constant trouble. Imagine a language like Mazatec, an Indian tongue of Mexico, in which there are four different registers of tone, and glides go up and down from one register to another. There are four words which we would write all alike as *tho*, but the one pronounced with a high tone means "will go out," the same consonants and vowel pronounced on a slightly lower tone means "a short period of time." On still a lower note the word means "goes out," a present tense, in contrast with the future, pronounced on the highest tone. This same combination *tho* pronounced on the lowest of the four tones means "a gunshot." Disregard for the tones would make any message unintelligible.

In the Mixtec language, spoken in the mountains of the State of Oaxaca, Mexico, there are three registers of tone, and each syllable must be pronounced on a high tone, a middle tone, a low tone, or on some glide between these tonal levels. There exist hundreds of contexts in which it is very easy to confuse the words. For example, the word *yuhu*, with a low tone on the first syllable and a high tone on the second, means "to fear." But the word *yuhu* with two high-tone syllables means "to kiss." Wrong tones in Mixtec could break up a romance in a very short time.

In the Trique language, also spoken in Mexico, there are apparently five levels of tones, and it is even easier to become confused. For example, a failure to put just the right waver in the voice in the

---

[2] These vowels are pronounced with a simultaneous escape of extra air through the vocal cords.

[3] The tones on the other words remain mid, high, and mid, respectively.

middle of the word *xan'an* changes "dove" to "skunk." Before one realizes it, he may be declaring that the Holy Spirit descended upon Jesus in the form of a skunk, and not a dove. The missionary translator among the Triques has had to be very careful to avoid all sorts of serious errors. Once he discovered that in a Bible story instead of saying, "Two rich men [i.e., Nicodemus and Joseph of Arimathea] asked for the body of Jesus," he was really declaring that two demons were asking for the soul of Jesus. This latter meaning would be the one more readily understood by the people, for what rich man would want the body of a dead man anyway? On the other hand, they could readily see how the demons might want Jesus' soul; for according to their beliefs the evil spirits are constantly spying on the souls of men in order to capture them.

Not all the difficulties which beset the translator consist of queer sounds; some of the problems involve strange grammars. It is not always easy to remember that if you want to make a negative statement in Mongbandi, a Sudanic language of northern Congo, the correct way is to repeat the verb at the end of the sentence. Hence, "He went home, went" is not an emphatic declaration that he returned home, but actually means that he did not go home. In order to be perfectly explicit about such a negative statement, one can use an emphatic form, which consists of repeating the verb twice at the end of the sentence, for example, "He went home, went, went!" This makes it absolutely certain that he did not go home. It, of course, does not mean that a stutterer cannot speak Mongbandi, but it does not pay to stutter on the verb at the end of the sentence, unless one is in a negative mood.

Even the simplest phrases may provide considerable trouble for the translator. In the Huastec language of central Mexico the phrase "in him verily is the love of God perfected" (I John 2:5) cannot be reproduced in this grammatical form. In Huastec there is no ambiguous preposition such as "of," which has more than a score of meanings in English and which reflects an almost equally ambiguous construction in the Greek. The translator must find some other way of expressing the same thought. In the first place, he must decide whether in this verse God is the object of the process of loving or is the one who does the loving, for in Huastec these two ideas are expressed quite differently. Most people agree that in this phrase "the love of God" refers not to God's loving people, but to their loving Him. But once this difficulty in interpretation is resolved, the translator is still faced with the problem of treating the passive expression "is perfected." In English the connotation is somewhat different from the Greek, for in the original the meaning is "to finish, to accomplish, to bring to completeness." But in order to describe the process of "bringing to completeness" a person's "love of God," one must say in Huastec, "He has really come to love God." Such a phrase may seem quite a distance removed from a literal translation of the Greek, but it is the closest equivalent in Huastec; and a translation which reproduces the original in the closest equivalent form in another language is a correct translation.

Many translation problems are made acute by virtue of the fact that one cannot find in other languages the types of words which correspond to our "parts of speech," e.g., nouns, verbs, prepositions, adjectives, etc. Such a phrase as "preached the baptism of repentance unto the remission of sins" (Mark 1:4) is difficult to translate because in so many languages words such as "baptism," "repentance," and "remission" (in Greek this is just the common word "forgiveness") are not nouns, but verbs, for they designate processes and not objects which can be seen or touched. As verbs they require subjects and the grammatical treatment which verbs have. How then is one to combine the meanings of these words in verb expressions? Even the phrase "baptism of repentance" is complicated enough. What is its precise meaning? Certainly, it is not the "baptism" which belongs to "repentance," but rather, it is the "baptism" which is characterized by "repentance." This being the case, repentance must precede baptism. As for the relationship of "forgiveness" (or "remission") and "sins," we may say that "sins" are the object of the process of forgiveness, or if we prefer to use a passive verb expression "be forgiven," then the "sins" would be the subject. The entire expression could then be rendered, "preached that people should repent and be baptized so that their sins should be forgiven." To some people this type of rendering may seem even clearer and more precise than the usual English translation; but the translator does not substitute verbs for nouns simply for the sake of diversity or novelty; he does make such changes when they are required by the grammatical "laws" of the language in question. A translation must conform to the grammatical tradition of the language (whether this is formulated in textbooks or passed on by the oral tradition of usage), but in any case a translation in order to be effective must represent the way people speak.

We need to be very careful when we become supercritical of other languages, for we are likely to discover some things equally unusual and indefensible in English. It may seem that the Shilluks of the Sudan are lacking in judgment when they say "good bad" to mean "very good." But English is no less strange in the use of "terribly good," for how can something be "terrible" and "good" at the same time? Or compare the phrase "good and bad" in the declaration, "Why, he isn't just bad, he's good 'n bad." For the proper meaning we often depend on a special intonation of the voice, and extra stress on the word "good." But this kind of usage is no less and no more illogical than the Shilluk "good bad." In fact, there is very little that is logical about many of our idioms. Who are we to speak about logic when we explain such idioms as "bees in his bonnet" and "bats in the belfry" as meaning that someone is "nuts"? Why should we complain because in some Bantu languages of central Africa there is no singular form of the noun "fleas," when we insist that "oats" should always be plural? Furthermore, whoever saw just one flea in Africa? Even on a practical level these Africans should score a point.

Not all the exasperating difficulties which beset the translator are caused by tongue-twisting sounds and confusing grammars; so many of the problems arise from profound differences in the lives and customs of peoples. In some ways aboriginal peoples are somewhat closer to the culture of Bible times than we are. In many primitive parts of the world water drawn from open wells, oxen treading out grain, millstones moved by donkeys, oil lamps, and sheepfolds can be more readily understood than in our own machine-age society. Nevertheless, there are serious problems, especially for the translator who works closely with his native helpers and seeks to have them understand the message as one meant for them.

Some things in the Scriptures strike native helpers as very foolish. One Maya preacher protested when he heard that Peter offered to build three little shelters—one each for Moses, Elijah, and Jesus. "Didn't Peter know," this translation helper inquired, "that it is much simpler to build one large shelter than three small ones?" Peter's apparent ignorance of building matters bothered this young Maya man.

Again, native peoples sometimes jump to wrong conclusions. They see parallels with their own culture and reinterpret the Scriptures accordingly. Some of the Aztecs of Guerrero, Mexico, volunteered to explain how the angels ministered to Jesus after His temptation in the desert. "Why, it was just like a rich landowner with his gunmen bodyguard," they declared, much to the surprise of the missionary. But a good man out in a lonely place in the mountains of Guerrero would need a bodyguard—that was certain!

In many instances there are such complete contrasts in environment that even the best of explanations seem pitifully inadequate. How can one talk of mountains and rivers among the Mayas of Yucatan? On that flat, limestone, wooded plain most Mayas have never seen a hill more than two hundred feet high, and streams, even during torrential rains, never run more than a few yards before the water disappears beneath the surface and flows in great underground channels. The Shipibos of the jungles of eastern Peru likewise have their troubles in understanding some parts of the Biblical account. Living as they do in the midst of a vast, impenetrable jungle along one of the great tributaries of the Amazon, they cannot conceive of a wilderness, in the sense of some place where practically nothing grows. In translating Matthew 4 the best equivalent of the wilderness is "a place where no one lives," but, after all, this means off in the forest. What disturbs the Shipibos, however, is not that John the Baptist should have preached out in the forest, but that Jesus should have gotten hungry out there. It seems incredible to the Shipibos that Jesus would not have known enough to kill some animals or at least to have found some fruits or edible herbs. The stories of the Bible almost never appear to have happened in the very next town, for environmental and cultural features are so different. And yet the Good News should come in such a form that it will speak intimately to people in order that they may realize the message is for them—not just for their neighbors.

After mastering the sounds and grammar of a language, becoming familiar with the cultural problems (including the strange contrasts with and similarities to our own manner of life and thinking), and after becoming somewhat fluent in the use of the native language so that one can discuss all sorts of topics, then one can take up really serious translation work. As the first step in the translating procedure, the translator must study over a passage, using several good scholarly commentaries. Even the most familiar passage deserves consideration.

After investigating the meaning of a passage by carefully consulting adequate authorities, the translator usually formulates some tentative translation of the passage. Quite often he tries to keep his translation helpers from even knowing that he has worked out such a rough preliminary draft, for they are sometimes inclined to agree to anything the missionary has done, even though they do not understand it completely. This tentative draft is used only to explain the meaning of the passage, and he wants to obtain the better form of the phrase from the lips of his helpers. If the translator relies too much on his own wording of the translation, the resultant translation is too likely to be wooden and include many "foreignisms" from his own speech. These preliminary suggestions are designed to stimulate discussion among the translation helpers, who often want more information about the historical setting before they can be satisfied that their understanding is sufficient to work out an intelligible translation.

The translation helpers working on the Tzeltal New Testament for their rapidly growing church in southern Mexico often discuss a verse for an hour or more. Sometimes they even wait for a day or so to consult with other members of the congregation. But when finally some difficult phrase in the Pauline Epistles has been clearly expressed in their language, smiles spread over their faces, their eyes gleam with understanding and appreciation, and they exclaim, "That is just the way Paul said it."

Not all men on a translating committee are of equal importance, and not all have the same kind of contribution to make. One man may have a thorough mastery of native religion, another may be able to give the right grammatical turn to the phrase, still another may be able to discover some new metaphor or simile to describe new spiritual experiences, but each has something to offer.

The translator must never forget for a moment that each word and each phrase, though it speaks of the Good News, which is essentially new and in a new setting, must nevertheless be expressed by words which come from old ways of life and have their meanings established in old beliefs. A word for "spirit" will bear something of the pagan belief in spirits, a term for "God" will carry over something of ancient tradition about the Creator, and "sin" will be understood at first as it reflects or contrasts with native concepts of social taboo.

Frequently the translator is indebted to pagan shamans for some of the most important terms. For years Efrain Alphonse tried to find the Valiente name for "God." Many of the people did not know the word, and others refused to give it. Though there was a belief in a beneficent Creator, His name was too sacred to be known by the uninitiated. On one occasion, Mr. Alphonse went with some of his Valiente helpers to visit an old medicine woman back in the recesses of the tropical forest of Bocas del Toro. After being ushered into the presence of this greatly revered but hideous old woman, they answered at length the many questions which she asked. Finally she began to chant and sing, and as her voice rose higher and higher, she shouted out in trancelike ecstasy so that all could hear, "These men are talking about Ngobö, the God of heaven and earth. Listen to them!" Here was the name "Ngobö," the very word which Mr. Alphonse had been seeking for so many years. It came from the lips of a native diviner and sorceress, but all agreed that this was the name of God, and throughout the years it has been used by the Valiente Christians.

There are times when the translator finds strange mixtures of native legend with traces of Christian terms and concepts. The Tzeltals of southern Mexico in the area of Oxchuc pin their faith on St. Thomas, whom they worship in yearly drunken fiestas. It was St. Thomas who was supposed to have given them corn; and once when he walked through their land, wherever his staff touched the earth a bubbling spring gushed forth. They believe that God made the earth, but at present He is distant and evil in His intent to destroy men. In fact, He is believed to have made counterparts for men and to have them ready to send to the earth to take men's places. Only the intercession of St. Thomas keeps the wrath of God from descending upon mankind. Furthermore, they conceive of the world as flat and held up by four pillars, to one of which the Antichrist is chained. His struggling to get loose in order to destroy mankind causes frequent earthquakes, but it is St. Thomas who first chained the Antichrist and who keeps him chained. Jesus enters into the people's thinking only more or less incidentally, principally as the one who was so angered at having been tied up by the Jews that He sent a universal flood to destroy mankind. It is no wonder that in the midst of so many utterly false conceptions, the translator

must be especially careful to make certain that the people understand fully the significance of each phrase and sentence.

The missionary usually understands quite well how to deal with
distorted stories and perversions of truth, for the antidote consists
in simply explaining the truth in a positive manner as it is revealed
in the Word of God. However, there are some native reactions
which the missionary at first seems incapable of understanding.
When missionaries were telling some Chols in southern Mexico how
John the Baptist, a good and just man, was jailed and cruelly
killed by Herod because he told the truth, the people broke out in
riotous laughter. This laughter did not signify a callousness of
feeling, as one might think. They laughed because they felt so sorry
for John. At funerals the people do not cry—rather, they express
their deep sympathy by laughing heartily so that they will not cry.
At times, however, they cry for joy. The translation helper who
finally finished the translation of the Gospel of Matthew began to
cry as the last verse was completed.

Translation helpers are indispensable; they have mastered the
rich resources of the native language and the culture. Once they
understand what is meant by the Biblical phrase, they can usually
give a satisfactory equivalent, for languages are not as barren and
poverty-stricken as some have imagined. However, one must make
certain that these helpers do understand fully. The Chol translator
realized that the phrase "shutteth up his bowels" (I John 3:17)
would not be properly understood as meaning "has no compassion,"
so he suggested "shut up his heart." But the helpers could explain
that this phrase would not be correct, for "to shut up his heart" is a
Chol idiom meaning "to have an epileptic fit." The equivalent Chol
phrase is "he who doesn't give anything."

The translator's objective is to discover with the aid of his
collaborators those intimate resources of spiritual experience which
are revealed in meaningful language. In his search for these rich
lexical treasures he experiences some of the most thrilling aspects

of his work. The more or less prosaic verse, "The way of peace have
they not known" (Romans 3:17), becomes in Chol, "They have not
known the road of the quiet heart." The experience of the new
Christian converts reflects fascinating developments in words and
meanings. The Chols describe the first three steps in the Christian
life as "answering the Word," "learning the Lord," and "entering
into Christ." A person's first sympathetic response to the gospel is
called "answering the Word." His rejection is described conversely
as "passing by the Word." As he receives instructions in this new
faith, he is spoken of as "learning the Lord"; and the experience of
conversion, at which time he identifies himself completely as a
disciple of the crucified Saviour, is called "entering into Christ."
This last phrase sounds as though it came from the very pages of
the Pauline Epistles, but it is a completely native expression, coined
by the Chols to describe their vital relationship to Jesus Christ.

Spiritual experiences are not a series of isolated, inexplicable
events, without relationship to one another, but the nature of these
relationships can and should be indicated. In English the words
"repentance," "salvation," "conversion," and "peace" have a somewhat empty theological sound to many people, but the equivalent
phrases in Mazahua, spoken in the high mountains to the east of
Mexico City, reflect vividly the spiritual growth of the fiercely
persecuted Christians. "Repentance" is "turning back the heart";
"salvation" is "healing the heart"; "conversion" is "changing the
heart"; and "peace" is "resting in the heart."

In our complacent living we frequently miss the spirit which
characterizes so many of the dramatic, moving events of such books
as the Acts of the Apostles. But Indian Christians like the Tzeltals,
who in about a year and a half grew in numbers from a mere hand-
ful to a congregation of more than one thousand, and all this
despite severe persecution, know full well the meaning of the 14th
chapter of Acts. Witnessing in hostile towns, being stoned and
threatened, and even being left as dead are all happenings which
these Tzeltals can understand from personal experience. Angry

saloonkeepers, embittered by their loss of trade due to the effects of the gospel, burned down the native-built, thatch-roofed church; but there in the smoldering embers the band of near-by Christians, who had come to rescue the little hand organ and the benches, knelt and prayed that God would forgive those who in their fanaticism and ignorance had destroyed the church which they had built at so much cost in labor and material resources. Enemies might destroy the building, but they could not destroy the work of the Spirit of God among these formerly debauched, poverty-stricken people.

We take it for granted that people will give some respect to women. This is so much a part of our culture and way of life that it produces a kind of shock to find people who suddenly come to realize or admit that women have souls, even as men do. Formerly the Chols believed that women had no souls, or at least their souls were of such a distinctly inferior quality that women were not even buried in the same cemetery with men. Religion was only for men, and in some pagan rites the presence of women and children was strictly prohibited. But the coming of the gospel has changed all this. The Good News is for women as well as men, for the people have seen that the Spirit of God can work in the hearts of women too. Even the children, instead of being driven away, are brought up to the front of the church so they can hear and understand.

A book such as the Epistle of James is almost buried in our Bibles, but one family of Chols found in it the answer to a bitter family feud. Four brothers were fighting over inherited land, but at the advice of the missionary they read James' practical letter, designed for just such problems. Each man felt convicted in his heart. Then the women were called in, and again and again the book was read over. Finally, they prayed and asked the forgiveness of God and of one another. Peace was restored to a divided household through the reading of a letter written almost two thousand years ago.

The Tarascan Indians, dwelling around the shores of picturesque

Lake Patzcuaro in the green mountains of Michoacán, Mexico, seemed impervious to the message of Good News. To resist the oppression of feudal exploitation these Indian people had erected a high wall of cultural isolation. Missionaries working among them had made it a practice to conduct family devotions in English, but one day a Tarascan in the house asked them, "What are you doing?"

"Why—we are praying," they explained.

"Oh, you are reciting," he replied, for the English sounded like the meaningless Latin liturgy which he had heard at times in the far-off cathedral.

"Oh no! We are praying," the missionaries insisted. But the poor man could not comprehend.

At last, in order to make sure that he understood, they said, "You see, we are just talking with God. That's all. Just talking to God."

"Indeed?!" he exclaimed. "Oh please, talk to God in my language so I may listen in!"

CHAPTER 3

THORNS AND
THISTLES

There is an impression among some people that Bible translating is really quite an easy task, but these persons have not reckoned with the troublesome thorns and thistles which beset the translator at every turn. They presume that all one has to do is to ask natives for the right words and then proceed to write them down, but one can never take anything for granted. One missionary assumed that his helpers were giving him the right words, but in the Beatitudes they failed to understand the meaning of the Spanish *bienaventurados* "blessed," "fortunate," or "lucky"; and as a result the translation into one of the Indian languages of Latin America read literally, "Lucky in gambling are the poor in spirit . . .; lucky in gambling are those who mourn . . ." etc. The Indian helpers knew the Spanish word *bienaventurados* in only the one sense of "lucky," and they were happy over the prospects of material rewards for the poor humble hearers of Jesus' words.

Literal translations sometimes turn out ridiculous. In one language of Latin America the translator thought he was describing an image coming to life when he gave a literal rendering of "gave breath to the image" (Revelation 13:15), but what he actually said was, "He made the image stink." In another instance the natives were amazed at the recorded patience and long-suffering of the Lord, for according to the 26th chapter of Matthew in their New Testaments a repentant woman "broke a stone jar of ointment"

43

on Jesus' head. A strange way indeed to express gratitude! In still another case the literal translation of "birthday" (Mark 6:21) meant that Herod threw a drinking party for the leading men of the land on the very day he was born—an incredible stunt, so the people thought, but their mythical heroes were credited with equally amazing exploits at an early age and so they were ready to believe the mistranslation—but only as a fable.

Can you blame one group of Indians in Latin America for being disgusted with Paul when they read in their Scriptures that he talked of "leading a wife around like an ox" (I Corinthians 9:5)? The translator overlooked the right word "to lead by the hand" or "to accompany," and had thoughtlessly used a term which meant only "to lead around like some unruly animal."

Some literal renderings fail to provide the proper meanings, for they are interpreted purely in a material sense. For example, the Valientes of Panama would only understand "stiff-necked people" as those who were afflicted with severe paralysis or rheumatism of the neck. Their equivalent is "holding-back people." That is to say, they constitute the intractable, disobedient people who will not be led, or even pushed—they just hold back in defiance. The San Blas Indians of Panama, a tribe a few hundred miles away from the Valientes, describe similar folks as "people with stopped-up ears." These two different metaphors are two equally good ways of describing rebellious, unco-operative people who insist on their own way.

Some literal translations mean practically nothing. They are incongruous words—nothing more. A translation for the "Holy Spirit" used for some time in one Sudanic language meant only "clean breath," and that meant nothing, for whoever saw a "clean breath"? The translators had looked at their Greek and discovered that the word *pneuma*, meaning "Spirit," also means "breath." They thought that "holy" could best be translated by "clean," since they had an idea that a word describing a state of being physically clean would readily suggest the meaning of holiness. This is an idea which people often embody in the pseudo-Scriptural quotation to the effect that "cleanliness is next to godliness." For this African tribe, being clean was simply unrelated and unrelatable to holiness. But this was not all. The very combination "clean breath" was unthinkable. In order for anything to be clean, these people insisted that it would certainly have to be visible, but a breath is not visible; and hence, how could it be regarded as clean? How could a thing be clean unless it were washable, and whoever heard of washing a breath? Missionaries tried desperately to teach the meaning of this expression, but they completely failed to get across the meaning which they had at first regarded as so immediately evident. So many metaphorical flowers which the translator seeks to grow in the language prove to be thistles and thorns.

To understand a strange culture one must enter as much as possible into the very life and viewpoint of the native people. Otherwise, a person will not realize how ridiculous it is to talk to Indians of southern Mexico about scribes who "devour widows' houses" (Mark 12:40). Their houses are often made with cornstalk walls and grass roofs, and farm animals do eat them when fodder gets scarce, so that people guard against hungry cows breaking in to eat down a house. "Devouring widows' houses" is no bold metaphor in some places, but a real danger. Hence the native reader wonders, "What were these 'scribes' anyway? Was this just a name for starved, ravenous cattle?" In such cases one must translate "destroy widows' houses."

Cultural contrasts do not prevent translating; they only point the direction which the equivalent phrase indicates. One cannot say to the Zanaki people along the winding shores of sprawling Lake Victoria, "Behold I stand at the door and knock" (Revelation 3:20). This would mean that Christ was declaring Himself to be a thief, for in Zanaki land thieves generally make it a practice to knock on the door of a hut which they hope to burglarize; and if they hear any movement or noise inside, they dash off into the dark. An honest man will come to a house and call the name of the person inside, and in this way identify himself by his voice. Accordingly, in the Zanaki translation it is necessary to say, "Behold, I stand at the door and call." This wording may be slightly strange to us, but the meaning is the same. In each case Christ is asking people to open the door. He is no thief and He will not force an entrance; He knocks—and in Zanaki "He calls." If anything, the Zanaki expression is a little more personal than our own.

Cultural parallels at times seem strangely different. On the drying fringe of the vast Sahara desert around the city of Ouagadougou, in French West Africa, the hardy Mossi people know nothing of ships, and certainly nothing of anchors. It would be folly to talk about "a sure and steadfast anchor for the soul" (Hebrews 6:19). To explain the word "anchor" one would need almost a paragraph, and if one insists on "heavy, pronged piece of iron for the soul," this would surely mean a grievous, cruel burden and would have no reference to spiritual safety or security. But the Mossi people have a perfect parallel in the word "picketting-peg." They have prized herds of horses and cattle, and they make it a practice to stake out their animals during the night, tying them to a picketting-peg. Hence the Mossi people read in their New Testament, "A strong and steadfast picketting-peg for the soul." This word "picketting-peg" is especially valuable, for the Mossi people recognize its metaphorical significance. One of their proverbs is, "A man does not tie a good horse to a bad picketting-peg."

In some instances there are simply no cultural parallels. Believe it or not, in some parts of the world people know nothing about gambling. Such a people are to be found among the Shipibos, whose villages are perched on the banks of the broad winding Peruvian tributaries of the Amazon, flowing like tangled, shiny ribbons through endless green. One could search in the Shipibo language forever and still not find a native term for "gamble." There is no such word, for the people do not have games of chance. How then is a person going to translate Mark 15:24, where the soldiers "cast lots" for the clothing of Jesus? One can only describe—even though very inadequately—what possibly happened. Hence, the Shipibo translation reads, "They shook little things to decide what each one should take." Of course, the phrase "shook little things" will need explanation, but this is also true of many things in the Bible.

In places where missionaries have been unaware of the cultural problems involved, serious errors have been made and have caused widespread misunderstanding. One translator in West Africa finally extracted a word which he thought meant "to save." For years he used it, only to discover at last that it meant merely keeping ragged clothes together—scarcely a fitting term to describe the redemptive salvation described in the Bible. To make matters worse, he used a word for "grace" which was used in casting curses upon people. He had explained "grace" as great spiritual power descending upon people, but in many cultures supernatural power is more often fearful and harmful, rather than good. The word which the missionary persisted in using was so taboo that people would utter the word only when others were not listening, for they did not want to be accused of witchcraft. Rather than proclaiming the grace of God, the missionary was extolling the power of black magic and the efficacy of God's curse.

Even more serious, however, than such flagrant mistakes is the tendency to make easy adaptations to native ideas. In one area of West Africa the word for "save" literally meant "to free." This seemed fine, for in the true sense of the word, salvation is a freedom— freedom from the power and guilt of sin. To the practical-minded natives, however, this freedom meant something quite different. Boys who went to school and learned to read and write were not obliged to work on the roads, nor were they forced into jobs as carriers for government officials, and some had no taxes to pay. The converts that worked at the mission station were free from forced labor and free from taxation. Hence, for most people, becoming a Christian and being "freed" had no spiritual significance. They thought only of political and economic freedom, and being associated with the missionary was the best means of obtaining this. For years the earnest preaching of consecrated missionaries had fallen on materialistic ears. These West Africans are essentially like the woman at the well in Sychar, who was interested in the living water in order that she should no longer be obliged to go daily to the well to draw. But Jesus led her from her materialism to an acknowledgment of spiritual need. The gospel message often begins with the expressions for purely physical objects, but it must lead men to spiritual truth. This was, unfortunately, what these missionaries in West Africa were unable to do because they could not speak the native language well enough.

There is a temptation for missionaries to want to manufacture hosts of new words, fashioning them to fit their own ideas. Of course, a great amount of word-forming must be undertaken, but it must not be done in the comfortable isolation of one's study. Words must be tested by constant usage. Otherwise, one may produce such a preposterous expression as occurred in one Indian language in Mexico. The translator wanted to render John 1:14, where the Word is spoken of as "full of grace and truth." He argued with himself that naturally "grace" would be a "gift," but in this context at least it would have to be more than a gift. He would call it "a gift of life," or more literally, "a living gift." However, when his native helper was questioned about this word, he confessed that he did not understand it. Finally he said, "Well, I guess it means 'chicken.'" The point was that the only living (or live) gifts which the people ever exchanged were chickens. Hence, for the natives this passage declared that the Word was "full of chicken and truth."

As a solution to some of the more complicated problems of translating, it is often possible to borrow some technical word from the trade language spoken in the area. But such borrowing cannot be done without careful investigation; for once words have been borrowed, they acquire new meanings from the native culture and not from the culture from which they have come. The Motilone Indians of Venezuela borrowed the Spanish word *purísima* "purest" from the phrase *María purísima* "purest Mary," but the word *purísima*

now means "devil" in the Motilone language. It may seem strange
that the Motilones should have so altered the meaning of the word
purísima, but the reason is not difficult to find. These Motilones
heard the Spanish speakers using the phrase *María purísima* in precisely the kinds of situations in which they as Motilones would call
upon their pagan deities. They could not conceive that the Spanish-
speaking people would be calling upon good spirits to aid them in
their questionable dealings, and so the Motilones concluded quite
reasonably that this word *purísima* was the name of the Spanish
devil.

A similar development occurred in one of the tribes on Luzon
in the Philippines. The natives borrowed the Spanish word *seguro*
"certain, sure" but with the meaning of "perhaps," which they interpreted from the actions of the Spanish-speaking people who used
this word *seguro* to back up their very dubious statements.

The superficial veneer of religious terminology in Latin America
can be readily recognized when one hears *gluria* (an adapted form
of Spanish *gloria* "glory") used in some places to designate a
drunken religious festival, or when one discovers that in the Isthmus
Zapotec of Mexico the word *dumingu* (a borrowed form of *domingo*
"Sunday") really means a dance, or when the Spanish word *ayuno*
"fasting" cannot be employed in the Bolivian Quechua translation
because it implies religious fasting until noon, to be followed by
riotous drinking, all in honor of some local saint.

For those who regard only English as capable of fine distinctions
of meaning, it may come as a shock to realize that other languages
are often much more explicit about certain things. In the Kpelle
language of Liberia the expression "my sheep follow me" (John
10:27) could be translated by three different expressions. However,
two of these expressions would bear quite the wrong connotations.
One of them would mean "follow me, but at a great distance." This
is true enough of many people who claim to be Christians, but this is
not what Jesus was saying. Another way of translating this phrase

would mean "to stalk" or "to chase after," with the implication of evil intent. The correct translation is the third, which means "follow behind a leader."

By emphasizing the differences between languages it is possible for one to gather the impression that languages never use the same metaphors. This would be quite wrong. A Tarahumara Indian woman in the high mountains of northern Mexico may talk about her husband as "my old man." The Valientes in Panama may say, "He burned him up," when they mean that someone was made angry. Such metaphors sound vividly familiar.

The Shipibo idiom "to have a heart" sounds familiar enough to us, but it not only includes all that would be implied by the corresponding English expression, but goes beyond that and indicates a state of being socially well integrated. For the Shipibos the heart is the center of the personality. In an ideal sense one who possesses a personality should be integrated with others in the tribal unit. In Shipibo society the greatest emphasis is not upon being an outstanding personality, but upon one's ability to blend well into the social structure—making one's contribution without being self-assertive. This ideal is thus expressed in the metaphor "to have a heart."

But what is a person going to do if there are no metaphors and no ready-made expressions? The answer is, "Describe!" This is done in all languages. The Huanuco Quechua language of Peru has no current expression for "do not tempt God" (Matthew 4:7). These people probably never thought of this problem in the Biblical sense, but the present translation admirably describes this situation by saying, "Don't push God to do what you want." This sentence means more than even the English "tempt God," for our word "tempt" implies too much the idea of inducing to sin, and the real point of Matthew 4:7 is that we should not try to force God.

In the Black Thai language of Indo-China there seemed no way of talking about the "new birth." The word "new" simply could not be used with "birth," but the missionaries did solve the problem by using the phrase "birth to receive a new heart." After all, this is the meaning of the "new birth." The emphasis is not upon being born twice, but being born with a new nature.

Missionaries can work out alphabets and analyze grammars in a relatively few years. But it takes many years to enter into the soul of the language—its rich storehouse of idioms. Wooden, soulless translations can be made in a short time, but translations which speak intimately to the people must employ the inner language of the heart—not the outer language of commerce and business. In the Uduk language of the Anglo-Egyptian Sudan it would be possible to translate mundanely the phrase "mind your own business," but the Uduk way of speaking is "sit in the shade of your own hut," that is, do not be a busybody, snooping into others' affairs. In the Ngok Dinka one could translate literally "walk after the fashion of this world" (Ephesians 2:2), but this would be so inferior to the correct equivalent "sitting in the place of this world." The word "walking" has no metaphorical connection with behavior, while sitting does. In the Valiente language one can speak of "after sundown" in translating "evening," but the appropriate Valiente phrase is "the spirit of the day." In Aymara, an Indian language in the wind-swept highlands of Bolivia, the shore of the lake constitutes the "lips of the lake." In Shipibo a "cloud" is literally "sky-smoke," while in the Goajiro language of northern Colombia one speaks of a clear sky as consisting of "blue clouds."

Many native idioms reflect various mythological beliefs. The Mossi in French West Africa say that an eclipse of the moon is "a cat eating the moon," but the Miskitos in Nicaragua insist that "the moon has hold of his mother-in-law"—and is apparently getting the worst of it. We must not imagine, however, that such idioms imply literal belief in such ideas. The San Blas Indians call leprosy "the disease of a serpent bite." They recognize very well indeed that leprosy is not caused by a serpent bite, but this idiom has stuck. Its scientific accuracy is no more defended by them than the expression "devil's food cake" is to be taken literally as reflecting our beliefs. Native idioms are not without a humorous touch. The Uduks, for example, call the Adam's apple "the thing that wants beer."

As we study more and more of a language and interpret it in the light of the culture which it represents and of which it is a living part, we can understand more easily those features of the language which at first may have seemed quite contradictory and impossible. The scattered bands of warring Motilones in the rugged mountains on the frontier of Colombia and Venezuela have a word *etokapa* which they use in three quite distinct senses: (1) to commit suicide, (2) to make corn cakes, and (3) to hatch out eggs. Such meanings apparently bear no relationship to one another, but the Motilone Indians insist, and rightly so, that the word *etokapa* used in these three distinct senses is one and the same word. As we study the Motilone culture, however, it becomes evident that there is a very close relationship between these words, for all three actions involve egg-shaped objects. When a person dies, his body is wrapped up in an egg-shaped package and buried in the floor of the hut to rot. Then after about three years the bones are dug up and are wrapped in another oblong package and stored away in a distant mountain cave. The corn cakes are molded by hand into egg-shaped lumps and then boiled. Of course, the third meaning of hatching out eggs is readily relatable to the first two. The basic meaning of this verb *etokapa* is "an action having to do with egg-shaped objects." Once this is understood, then the relationship of the apparently unrelated meanings becomes obvious.

There is a certain sense in which many languages possess a number of specific, concrete terms but lack general, abstract ones. For instance, in Shipibo there are different names for all kinds of animals but no word for animals in general. On the other hand, aboriginal languages also possess generic terms which include extensive areas of meaning. In Ngok Dinka the word *dhueen* includes everything from "goodness" through "generosity" and up to and including "prestige." Such an almost unbelievable combination of

ideas reflects, of course, the Dinka cultural setup, in which one
cannot treasure up material possessions, for rotting mold attacks
during the humid months of tropical downpours and innumerable
rodents pillage the stored grain. Since it is impossible to horde, one
is obliged to distribute generously to everyone. Then, in case of
need, one may call upon them so as to receive in turn. Wealth and
prestige are not dependent upon accumulated possessions, but upon
one's capacity to give things away. The one word *dhueen* embraces
all of this cultural pattern.

In foreign cultures there are always many features which appear
quite contradictory. When we learn that in the Quechua dialect of
Bolivia one must speak of the past as being ahead of one and the
future as being behind one, we might be inclined to accuse the
Quechuas of being stupid or of having a perverted philosophical
orientation. Nevertheless, the Quechuas are fully able to defend
themselves and their idioms. They argue, "Well, try to imagine, if
you will, in your mind's eye the past and the future. Which can
you see?" Our only possible answer is that we can see the past and
not the future. "Right," they agree, "therefore, the past must be
ahead of you and the future behind you." Our interpretation of the
past and future is based upon movement; theirs is based on perspective. One is as valid as the other.

But can you talk about a "rectangular circle"? "Of course not!"
anyone would say, but the Piro Indians in the jungles of south-
eastern Peru can use such a phrase and correctly so. The difference
is that the geometrical perspective of the Piros is just not ours. They
have a word *poprololu* which may be translated either as "square"
or "round." What it really means is that the sides of the figure are of
equal proportion, whether straight or curved. The word *gitpo* is
generally translated "circle," but it primarily defines an object
bounded by curved lines. The word *goshpotalu* means a rectangular or oblong object, but generally with right-angle corners.
Goshpotalgitpo (a compound word made up of the second and third
words listed above) does not mean "rectangular circle" as one might

suppose at first glance, but identifies an oblong object of symmetrical, curved sides. Actually, none of these terms can be translated by any one term in English because the entire system of identifying geometric shapes is different from ours. Their system is equally as valid as ours and fully adequate to describe their elaborate and intricate designs painted on their pottery, clothing, and faces. The fact that the system is different from ours is no basis for depreciating it.

The more we assimilate of different cultural perspectives the more readily and more fully can we appreciate the idioms of other people. In the Yipounou language of the Gabon the equivalent of "they sent him away empty" (Mark 12:3) is "they sent him away holding his hands." The servant who was sent to carry back to his master some of the fruits of the vineyard was turned away without a thing. One can readily visualize this abused servant departing, holding nothing but his own hands. These are the word pictures which give life to the message.

Some of the word pictures of the Bible have grown dim to us because we no longer understand the culture out of which they have come. The phrase "sealed with the promised Holy Spirit" (Ephesians 1:13) is one of these. To so many persons "sealed" suggests "canned" and "preserved," while the Biblical idea is the confirmation of ownership. The Ngok Dinkas do not employ seals to indicate ownership nor do they confirm an agreement by using sealing wax and a signet ring, but they do mark ownership of their cattle by branding them. When speaking of the Christian's relationship to God, it is not enough to use the words "to brand," but this phrase has been expanded and enriched by the words "in the heart." Accordingly, Ephesians 1:13 reads, "You were branded in the heart by the Holy Spirit who was promised."

Words which in former days included bold figures of speech have often lost their meanings. This is true of the English word "hypocrite," which is a borrowing from Greek and originally meant "an actor." In the Malagasy language, however, the word for a hypocrite is fully understandable in terms of everyday life, for a hypocrite is "one who spreads a clean raffia carpet." The expression arises from the practice of some untidy housekeepers who happen to glance out, and seeing a visitor approaching up the path, hastily take down from the wall a clean raffia carpet and quickly spread it over the dirty, unswept floor. Hypocrites are regarded as specializing in this kind of rapid outward transformation, while remaining at heart their same dirty selves.

CHAPTER 4

GREEK AND
HEBREW
TREASURES

A carefully written letter from a devout lover of the Bible was received at the Bible House. In substance it read:

I would be so glad to help in the translating of the Bible, and so if you would send me a dictionary and a grammar of some of these primitive languages, I would be happy to dedicate my spare time to the translation of the New Testament.

The desire to be of service to those who do not have the Bible is commendable, but no translator can obtain meaningful results by simply following intricately devised grammatical rules and matching words from the average dictionary. The true Bible translator must be a profound student of the native language, with all its rich cultural implications, and of the Biblical languages, which he needs to study thoroughly in order to understand their historical setting.

No superficial knowledge of the Bible will suffice for the translator. Without thorough training he may discover that he is only passing on his own ignorance, based upon erroneous interpretations of words. How many people there are who think that "taking the Lord's name in vain" refers to common profanity! Perhaps in a sense it does, but the meaning of the Old Testament is not that the Lord's name is unmentionable in oaths, but that one should not swear by

the Lord and then fail to perform one's promise. "Foreswearing" is
not cursing, but promising to do something in the Lord's name and
then failing to make good. The habit of using God's name had become so common and meaningless among the Jews that Jesus
warned people not to use God's name at all, for they were making
a mockery of their faith.

Some expressions in the Bible seem so perfectly obvious to us
that we do not take the time to examine them or to inform ourselves more fully as to their possible meaning. When we read about
"Simon the Cananaean" (Revised Standard Version), we take it for
granted that "Cananaean" refers to the land from which he came. A
close examination of this text in the Greek shows us that it is not
the land at all. The word is a transliterated Aramaic term which
means "zealot," that is, one who belonged to the rabid nationalist
party. Knowing this, we can understand more easily why this same
man is called "Simon Zelotes" in Acts 1:13 and "Simon the
Cananaean" in Matthew 10:4. In Acts we have the Greek translation
and in Matthew the Aramaic word borrowed into Greek. A man
like Simon, so well known for his strong anti-Rome politics, would
seem to some to be a liability for Jesus' political future. On the other
hand, Jesus chose Levi, a publican, who had been regarded as a
traitor to his own people by signing up with Rome to collect taxes
for them. Within the small group of Jesus' own disciples there were
these two men who represented opposite poles of political feeling
and action. Neither of these men would be likely to enhance Jesus'
political prestige, but He was obviously not courting earthly power
but proclaiming the kingdom of heaven.

There are those who read into the Scriptures a justification for
political haranguing of the multitudes. They argue, "But did not
Jesus instruct us to 'preach upon the housetops'? (Matthew 10:27).
Does not this imply shouting to the passing crowds in the streets
below?" It would be so in our society, but the words of Jesus were
addressed to the people of His day. What He meant was that His
disciples should take what they heard from Him in secret and

should speak to their neighbors about it, as in the cool of the evening the families of the close-fitting houses gathered on near-by flat house-tops to rest and chat. Jesus was not thinking of a political gathering, but of one neighbor telling another, witnessing of the faith that had become an intimate part of his life and something which he wished to share with his closest neighbor.

Some misinterpretations of the Bible result from changes in the meanings of words. In I Thessalonians 4:15 the words "we which are alive and remain . . . shall not prevent them which are asleep" seem to imply some peculiar doctrine of interference until we realize that this use of the word "prevent" is a very old one, reflecting its meaning in its original Latin value, namely, "to come ahead of." Such a verse should be translated as "shall not precede them which are asleep." In II Thessalonians 2:7 we encounter the strange rendering, "he who now letteth will let, until he be taken out of the way." This verse contains an old English word, which is only preserved in the legal phrase "let or hindrance" and in the tennis expression "a let ball." However, for most people the common usage is "net ball," not "let ball." This old word "let" meant "to hinder" or "to restrain." Hence a "let ball" is a hindered ball in tennis, but since it is usually hindered by the net, we generally speak about a "net ball." But in II Thessalonians 2:7 the meaning is that the One who now hinders or restrains shall continue to do so until He is taken out of the world.

Some mistranslations of the King James Version resulted from inadequate knowledge of the originals. This does not mean that the scholars who prepared the King James Version were not fully abreast of the Biblical knowledge of their day. It only means that during the succeeding centuries we have been privileged to learn much more about the meanings of words and the significance of certain grammatical forms. In John 20:17 the King James reads "Touch me not," but the more correct translations read "Do not hold me" or even "Do not keep holding onto me." It was formerly thought that the different tenses of the Greek verb refer only to time, but we know now that they often signify different aspects or kinds of action. In this verse the Greek has a present form, which means that one is to cease doing what he is doing. If the verb had been an aorist, a different grammatical form of the verb, it would have meant not to do something in the future, that is, something not being done at the time. Not knowing about this subtle distinction, the translators of the King James did the best they could, but their translation has resulted in many rather fanciful explanations of how Jesus could not be touched because He had not yet presented Himself in heaven, but how He did so in just a few minutes of time, since in Matthew 28:9 we read of Jesus meeting the women on their return to Jerusalem, and there the text says specifically that they touched His feet.

Many subtle distinctions in the original languages are difficult to translate in every instance, but whenever possible they should be properly treated. In Matthew 6 one encounters two forms of the verb meaning "to worry, to be anxious" (in the King James "take thought for"). In Matthew 6:25 the form of the verb means "do not continue to worry about." This is the present form of the verb, similar to the form occurring in John 20:17, noted just above. After Jesus has given His encouraging discourse on God's provision for the needs of His children, He then ends with a different form of the verb. In Matthew 6:34 the verb means "now don't worry any more about these things in the future." He begins His message by urging His followers to stop worrying and ends by assuming that they have ceased to worry and hence admonishes them never to worry again. In English translations it is awkward to convey all of this meaning without cumbersome phrases which tend to overtranslate the original, but in many other languages one can perfectly match certain of these intensely meaningful distinctions of the Greek.

There are some passages in the Scriptures in which the King James Version seems to suggest distinctions which are not to be found in the original. In Mark 1:4 one reads of the "remission of sins." For certain people the word "remission" has been regarded as a technical theological term, indicative of something rather different from "forgiveness." But in the Greek the word translated here as "remission" is just the common word "forgiveness." Accordingly, most of the more recent translations into English use the familiar and more meaningful term "forgiveness."

A close study of more modern translations and the careful reading of scholarly commentaries will help the Bible translator avoid many of the mistakes which would otherwise arise because of his limited understanding based on the traditional renderings. But there is really no substitute for at least some knowledge of the original languages. This knowledge must not be superficial or based upon apparent, but unreliable, etymologies or associations between words. Some people have argued that the Greek word *katabolê* could not possibly mean "foundation" or "establishment" (John 17:24 and Ephesians 1:4) since its constituent parts mean "down" (*kata-*) and "to throw" (*bol-*). They have insisted that such a word would have to mean "destruction." Hence they argue that "since the foundation of the world" in John 17:24 and elsewhere should be rendered as "since the destruction of the world." The reasons for this interpretation lie in certain fanciful ideas about various pre-Adamic dispensations, but from the standpoint of the Greek there is simply no justification for the meaning of "destruction." The meanings of words cannot be determined by pulling apart their components. If that were so, we would be hopelessly lost in attempting to explain the difference in meaning between the English nouns *up-set* and *set-up*, both having the same constituent parts, but meaning something quite different.

Some would-be students of Greek have insisted that the adjective *aiônios* must mean only "of an age" or "for an age" because it is related to the noun *aiôn* "age." But here again, the meaning is not determined by the similarities which a foreigner can discover between words, but by the manner in which these words are used by native speakers of the language. In John 3:16 the Scriptures are not speaking about "life for an age" but "eternal life." The student of the Bible must not dictate the meaning of the original words, but discover their meaning from their Biblical contexts and from their wide use in non-Biblical sources. Only by this means would he ever be able to recognize the fact that the Greek word *charis* can mean "beauty," "kindness," "grace," "gift," and "thankfulness." Similarly, the student of Hebrew finds the same root *nbl* in words meaning "shriveled," "wasted away," "crumbled to dust," "foolish," "impious," "carcass," "corpse," and "idol."

As anyone studies foreign languages there are many tempting etymologies which may suggest truths, but which may not be historically valid. This is true of some popular treatments of the Greek word *ekklêsia* "church." It is quite true that the Greek word comes from two roots which mean literally "called out." Many preachers have made use of this fact to point out helpful spiritual implications, and yet by New Testament times the word carried no such denotation as "called out." It was simply the word for "assembly" or "congregation." It so happened that in the Greek city-states an assembly of the citizenry resulted from the people being called out of their city and summoned from their farms to participate in such gatherings. Even though the etymology of the word remains, its real meaning is just "assembly," and a Greek-speaking person of New Testament times would be no more inclined to understand *ekklêsia* in its original etymological value of "called out" than we today would recognize "God be with you" in "good-by," which, as we may learn from the dictionary, was derived from the longer phrase.

We must not think, however, that because there are dangers in the misunderstanding of words, we should abandon the idea of probing the depths of lexical lore in order to understand and appreciate the Scriptures more fully. Nothing could be more untrue. The translator's work is immeasurably enriched by sound examination of the original languages. In fact, he must constantly make reference to the original languages since in direct proportion as he separates himself from the Greek and Hebrew by intervening languages, by the same degree does he tend to depart from the original meaning and lose the richness of the divine revelation.

Just a few Greek and Hebrew words will indicate something of the treasures which are in store for the one who will only go in search for them.

In Greek there are two words which are translated as "covenant," "contract," or "agreement." These are *diathêkê* and *synthêkê*, but only the first of these occurs in the New Testament. What, then, seems to be the reason why the Scripture writers employed only *diathêkê*? Is there some subtle distinction which we miss in English? There is. Both of these words may be used to denote a "covenant" or "contract," but by the use of *diathêkê* we understand that one person alone initiates the agreement and draws up the terms. It remains for others to accept or reject. It is for this reason that *diathêkê* is used to mean a "will" or "testament" since the one who wills his property is the one who takes the initiative in determining the contract, and he is the one who stipulates the conditions and rewards. In working out a *synthêkê* there are possibilities for arguments, concessions, compromise, and final bargaining by both parties, but in a *diathêkê* only one party to the covenant is responsible for its form. In this distinction lies one of the most profound truths of Scriptures. God is no one to be bargained with, for He will not settle for anything less than the best for man. In non-Christian religions man is often regarded as a shrewd merchant with a record-keeping god or spirit. Man is thought to be able to pit his cleverness against the inattention of a deity in order to procure supernatural benefits at bargain rates. But there is no such basis for dickering with the God of Scripture. It is He who has established the covenant. We are the heirs. We can deny our sonship and waste our inheritance in riotous living, but God's plan will not be cheapened or His sovereignty infringed by clever men who refuse to accept the covenant of grace, established in the counsel of God and ratified by the death of His Son, for His was the blood of the new covenant (*diathêkê*, I Corinthians 11:26).

The two most famous synonyms in Greek are *agapaô* and *phileô*, words which are both translated "love," and yet they denote quite different phases of this most powerful of all emotions. It has been said that *agapaô* refers to "the love of God" and *phileô* is only "the love of men." But this distinction is only a very small part of the difference, and as such is in itself incorrect. Both of these words may convey intense emotion or may be relatively weak in their meanings. These words do not indicate degree of love, but kinds of love. *Agapaô* refers to love which arises from a keen sense of the value and worth in the object of our love, and *phileô* describes the emotional attachment which results from intimate and prolonged association. That is why in the Scriptures we are never commanded to "love" with the word *phileô*. Even when husbands and wives are instructed to love one another, the word *agapaô* is used, for it is impossible to command that kind of love which can arise only from intimate association. On the other hand, the saints are admonished to appreciate profoundly the worth and value in others, and *agapaô* is used to convey this meaning. All Christians are not necessarily to have sentimental attachments for one another (*phileô*). This would be impossible, for our circle of intimate friends is limited by the nature of our lives. But we can all be commanded to appreciate intensely the worth of others. When "God so loved the world" (John 3:16) it was not with any sentimental attachment which He might have had for sinful mankind, but He looked upon men with the eyes of grace. He saw in men the worth which they had as His children, even when they persisted in their sinful rebellion. This was the redemptive love of *agapaô*.

The meaning of one difficult passage hinges primarily upon the meaning of one Greek word. When we read "A good tree bringeth not forth corrupt fruit, neither doth a corrupt tree bring forth good fruit" (Luke 6:43), we are puzzled at first, for we know quite well that many an old, rotten peach tree has still produced some delicious peaches and some very fine-looking trees produce very poor fruit, some of which may spoil while still on the tree. What then can be the meaning of this word "corrupt" (Greek *sapros*)? One clue is to be found in the use of this same word in the parable of the fishes which were taken in the great net (Matthew 13:47, 48). The good fish were put into vessels, but the bad fish (the Greek adjective *sapros* is used) were thrown away. Certainly, this net did not draw in rotting fish, but rather inedible fish. This word *sapros* designates inedible varieties. Now we may apply the word to the trees and the fruit. Some seedling trees, despite their beautiful appearance, produce inedible fruit. It is the very nature of the tree, and such a tree could not produce good fruit if it wanted to. In contrast, the tree which naturally produces edible fruit cannot produce the bitter inedible fruit, which is characteristic of some unbudded fruit trees. The proper understanding of this word *sapros* "corrupt" makes the entire parable take on new meaning. Men produce fruit in accordance with their basic nature. The outward appearance is unimportant; only the fundamental character counts. Hence, to produce the fruit of the Spirit, we must be ingrafted with the life of the Spirit of God. We must have a new nature. As Jesus expressed this truth to Nicodemus, we must be born anew.

Some words become encrusted with our own linguistic tradition, and only by returning to the Greek and Hebrew can we recapture the fundamental significance of the message of God's revelation. One group of such words comprises "saint," "holy," "sanctify," and "sanctification." With only an understanding of the connotations of these words in English we gather the impression that the Bible is talking about a kind of sanctimonious do-nothing religion, a twiddling of the thumbs in some pious atmosphere, the innocuous mumbling of well-memorized prayers, or the uninspired repetition of standard clichés which gain one the reputation of being spiritually minded, even though the heart may be wholly occupied with things of this world. Whatever positive significance we discover in these words is related simply to moral goodness, and reflects little of the holy grandeur which surrounds them in Hebrew and Greek. The *sanctification*

Hebrew root *qdsh* and the Greek root *hag-* are not just synonyms for "good." Their primary significance is "set apart, consecrated, dedicated to the exclusive service of God." For us who have endeavored to defend the Christian religion in a humanistic society by emphasizing its ethical values, it comes as somewhat of a shock to find that one of the most crucial words in all the Scriptures is not primarily one of ethical content at all. It means "exclusive dedication to God." This truth becomes immediately apparent when we realize that the same Hebrew root is used in the words meaning "harlot" and "Sodomite." What were these poor creatures in pagan Semitic religion? They were devotees, consecrated to the sensual worship of their pagan deities. It is the old story of temple girls and boys, a practice still existing in some parts of the Orient, where people are dedicated to the gods for the purposes of sexual prostitution.

Where, then, did the Hebrew and Greek terms acquire the moral content which is reflected in our understanding of the corresponding words in English? The moral content comes from the nature of God and from the life which His worshipers are expected to live because they are consecrated to Him. We need to capture again the consciousness of that awesome holiness, which characterizes the majesty of God. This will save us from the "chummy sentimentality" which is so common in some people's talk about the Eternal and will exalt our concept of consecration, for our holiness must reflect His holiness or it is not true holiness, only self-imposed piety.

It is easy to misinterpret the Old Testament because we may have too restricted an idea of the meanings of the words. The Hebrew term *nephesh,* frequently translated as "soul," has several meanings, including "breath," "life," "mind," "living thing," "animal," "person," and "self" (in such a phrase as "I myself"). In Ezekiel 18:4 people have tried to read into the statement, "The soul that sinneth, it shall die," some implications that would seem to refer to the destruction of the soul itself. But the entire context and the meaning of this word *nephesh* is quite contradictory to any such interpretation. What Ezekiel meant was, "The person who commits sin—and no one else—shall be punished for it."

mercy

There are some words which cannot be explained by all the detailed comments of exhaustive dictionaries. One such word is the Hebrew term *ḥesed*, translated variously as "mercy," "pity," "kindness," "love," "loving-kindness," "goodness," "compassion," "steadfast love," and "grace." But these words only begin to point out the rich connotation of this Semitic term. It is the steadfast love of a king for his subjects and the heartfelt devotion of subjects for their king; the intense kindness of God for His people, and the loyal love of the people for their God. Some translators have rendered it as "covenant love," but this is too restrictive. It is the all-pervading emotion which binds God and man together and expresses itself in constant acts of mercy, kindness, and piety. Even then our best descriptions fall short of the full meaning of this word. We can only come to sense its significance as we read and reread the Law and the Prophets and there see how *ḥesed* describes the richness of mercy, love, and kindness which links God and man.

The translator who goes about his task faithfully and in so far as possible attempts to reckon with the Biblical context, taking into consideration all the historical background for the revelation of God's Word, will discover not only rich meanings in the striking passages of great theological import, but he will also find some of the greatest proofs of the Bible's authenticity in those little words and phrases which one passes by almost without noticing. In Mark 1:32 we might feel that the writer was unduly repetitious when he says, "when evening had come and the sun had set." Why two phrases when one would seem to be sufficient? But in that repeated and emphasized phrase we have the key to the picture of what happened that day. Jesus had gone into the synagogue of Capernaum to teach. A man with an unclean spirit had come in and had cried out in recognition of Jesus of Nazareth. Jesus commanded the spirit to come out of the man and he was healed, much to the amazement of the crowd. After the service in the synagogue Jesus went with some of His disciples to Peter's home, but it was not until that evening when the sun had set and hence the Sabbath day had passed that these conscientious observers of the Jewish law dared to bring to Him "all who were sick or possessed with demons." The fact that Jesus had healed a man on the Sabbath was not enough evidence that others should violate Sabbath regulations by seeking healing. One can picture these people waiting anxiously in their homes until finally the evening had come. Just as soon as the sun had set, they made all haste to bring to Jesus their sick and demon-possessed relatives and friends.

In Matthew 5:15 we are likely to accuse Jesus of hyperbole when He declares that men do not put a lamp under a bushel "but on a stand, and it gives light to all in the house." Knowing the kinds of small feeble lamps used in ancient times in the Jewish households it seems strange that He should have said, "to all in the house." "What about the other rooms of the house?" someone is likely to inquire. The truth of the matter is that Jesus was addressing Himself to the common people, most of whom lived in one-room houses. Certainly, few of them could afford the luxury of several oil lamps. Jesus was talking to men and women in words and phrases which reflected their very lives.

To most of us the number of "a hundred and fifty-three," which was the number of fish caught in the net along the shores of Galilee after the resurrection (John 21:4-14), seems incredibly trifling. We might be inclined to wonder why the writer had any interest in giving the number. When, however, we realize that in ancient times the number 153 was given as the total number of all the tribes and nations of earth, it is no wonder that the early church interpreted this passage as the assurance of success in fulfilling the great commission to bear the Good News to all men everywhere.

Words do not always carry the same meanings in one language as they do in another. How strange it seems to us that Jesus would address His own mother as "woman" after her request at the wedding in Cana of Galilee and again from the cross. Such a term seems to indicate severity in Jesus' own nature and appears to imply some reproof for the mother who had been so faithful to Him. This is because we do not realize that in the Greek of New Testament times the use of the word *gynai* "woman" implies both respect and endearment. In fact, the use of "woman" indicates more affection, than if Jesus had used the more formal word "mother." This may seem incredible to us, but we must never make the fatal mistake of judging other languages by our own.

Not only words and historical settings reveal hidden truths, but even grammatical forms may throw fresh light upon some otherwise unrecognized reality. For the ancient philosopher and priest of esoteric cults, steeped in the tradition of Classical Greek, the grammatical forms in the Lord's Prayer would seem almost rude. One does not find the optative forms of polite petition so characteristic of elaborate requests made to earthly and heavenly potentates. Rather than employing such august forms, the Christians made their requests to God in what seem to be blunt imperatives. This does not mean that Christians lacked respect for their heavenly father, but it does mean that they were consistent with a new understanding of Him. In the tens of thousands of papyri fragments which have been rescued from the rubbish heaps of the ancient Greek world, one finds the imperative forms used constantly between members of a family. When the Christians addressed God as "Father," it was perfectly natural therefore for them to talk to Him as intimately as they would to their own father. Unfortunately, the history of our own English language has almost reversed this process. Originally, men used "thou" and "thee" in prayer because it was the appropriate familiar form of address, but now these words have become relegated to prayer alone. However, to those who have not been raised in the atmosphere of the church and Sunday school such forms seem awkward and artificial. It is interesting to note how many people are beginning to pray to God with the pronoun "You." In doing this, they are following the New Testament principle, which makes little or no use of the high-flown artificial Asian style of Greek, but presents its sublime message in the words of common men. Repeatedly the Church is called upon to cast aside the shackles of a tradition abounding in words of empty meaning. Whenever it addresses itself to living men in living words, faith is made alive by the Spirit of God.

The Bible translator soon becomes profoundly aware of the essential unity of his task. He may have begun by thinking of the New and Old Testaments as separate compartments of revelation, but his judgment will soon be modified, for there are only four short books of the New Testament (Philemon, and I-III John) in which one does not find quotations from the Old. In Revelation there are more than 450 Old Testament quotations and allusions, and the books of Matthew, Acts, Luke, and Hebrews each have more than 100 quotations, often consisting of as much as several verses. The books which are most often quoted in the New Testament are Psalms (186 times), Isaiah (177 times), Exodus (91 times), Genesis (79 times), Ezekiel (63 times), and Jeremiah (55 times). In fact there are only four books of the Old Testament which are not quoted in the New: Ruth, Ezra, Ecclesiastes, and the Song of Solomon.[1] The unity of Scripture does not stop with quotations, for there are great themes which unite the sixty-six books of the Bible into one revelation. Words such as "covenant," "grace," "sacrifice," "love," "mercy," "redemption," "joy," "peace," "salvation," "holy," and "judgment" bind the Scriptures together in one indissoluble whole. A translator cannot correctly decide upon words for the New Testament without bearing in mind what he must use in the Old.

We must be careful not to think that translating is too easy a task, nor must we be unduly frightened by the magnitude of the many difficulties. Translating the Bible is not the work of a few weeks or months. It is the task of years, and often of a lifetime. However,

---

[1] These figures are based upon the Appendix to the Nestle Greek New Testament, 20th edition.

two of the most difficult problems in translating usually remain quite unnoticed by the amateur or the untrained student. One of these perplexing difficulties is what to do with Paul's long sentences. They are not utterly impossible in English, for we can have long, involved sentences with many dependent clauses though that is not our usual manner of speaking. However, in languages which are utterly different from Indo-European ones, the translator finds that he must often completely revamp the involved sentence structures which are so familiar in the writings of Paul. One receives the impression that this great missionary pioneer, founder of churches and apostle to the Gentiles, was at times so full of his subject that he simply could not find appropriate stopping places, and yet his sentences are not abnormally long in comparison with other Greek writers. Nevertheless, it is no easy task to take apart these linguistic monuments of clauses heaped one upon the other in intricately related positions and at the same time to preserve the meaningful relationships among these foundation truths of Christianity.

Another exasperating problem for the Bible translator and exegete is the Hebrew use of the tenses of the verb. Perhaps we should not even call the Hebrew forms different tenses, for they do not primarily signify different times of the action, but different kinds. Traditionally, the two principal sets of forms of the verb have been known as Imperfective and Perfective. And they correspond roughly to incomplete and complete action. Generally, the imperfective corresponds to our present and future tenses while the perfective is translated by our past, but there are many exceptions. Furthermore, when a perfective verb occurs in the first clause and the following clauses are joined by a Hebrew particle called *waw*, then the imperfective has the same value as the perfective in the first clause. Similarly, an initial perfective verb may be followed by imperfectives introduced by *waw*. Now, to make the situation even more complicated—when the prophet speaks of the future he always uses the perfective, that is to say, he speaks of the future as though it had already been accomplished. The Biblical interpreter is often confused, for it is hard to know when the writer is prophesying and when he is recounting the history of a people. For the most part the context makes it clear as to the meaning of the passage, but in some instances we are left with legitimate doubts, for we are unable to reconstruct the historical background with sufficient assurance.

The average reader of the Bible is likely to be troubled by differences in the manuscripts, which result in quite different translations of old familiar verses. When this happens our first reaction is generally a sense of loss. We have come to love the traditional rendering; and since it has been a part of our former religious experience, we assume that any change would only destroy the significance and spiritual content of the verse for us. When we read Romans 8:28 in the Revised Standard Version (1946), we find that "in everything God works for good with those who love him." We are told in a footnote that our older favorite rendering "all things work together for good" is a possible interpretation, but there is a sense in which we seem to prefer the older form, even as we feel more at home with old friends than with more recent ones. Jesus himself explained man's inevitable longing for tradition by the pointed parable about those who had drunk the old wine and did not appreciate the new wine, for they declared, "The old is better" (Luke 5:39). But we should not pass by these better attested renderings without examining them. It is possible that we may have missed some spiritual truth. While holding to our former understanding of a matter we may rob ourselves of rich insight. It is not enough for us to argue that we must of course accept the "better rendering" because it is more "scholarly" or more "scientific." Religion is so largely a matter of the heart that we are unlikely to accept new interpretations unless we test them by their value in the light of Christian experience. We should look at these two renderings of Romans 8:28 again. What is the basic difference? In the one, "All things work together for good," and in the other it is God who is working these things for our good. In the first there is a kind of blind fatalism which seems to imply an impersonal background to existence. In the second there is an emphatic declaration that a personal God is the basis of our Christian life and experience. The first interpretation sometimes leads to reckless exploits, the second provides the basis of quieting assurance.

In I John 5:18 we are accustomed to the translation, "We know that whosoever is born of God sinneth not; but he that is begotten of God keepeth himself, and that wicked one toucheth him not." It may be a surprise to find that in the Revised Standard Version this verse is translated, "We know that any one born of God does not sin, but He who was born of God keeps him, and the evil one does not touch him." The contrasts in meaning between these two translations are vast, but in Greek the only difference is the absence of a single small letter, making the difference between "himself" and "him." The older rendering states a truth which is manifestly contradicted by our experience and other Scripture. We as Christians are not able to keep ourselves. But we immediately recognize the truth of this newer rendering. We are not entrusted with the task of keeping ourselves, but "He who was born of God [that is, Jesus Christ] keeps us." This is the ministry of the resurrected Lord, who by His Spirit, sustains His redeemed. The grace of God does not stop with salvation, but becomes the basis of sanctification as well.

Some phrases in the King James Version are almost impossible to understand correctly since the Greek text which was available in the seventeenth century was so obviously faulty. In I Corinthians 8:7 we encounter the phrase "conscience of the idol." What can this mean? Does the Bible imply that an idol has a conscience? This would surely not be in keeping with the teachings of Scripture. It is similarly not "consciousness of the idol." In certain manuscripts two Greek words were confused; one meaning "conscience" and the other "experience." Once we understand this, the textual problem is settled; and we can fully appreciate the great improvement in the Revised Standard Version, "But some, through being hitherto accustomed to idols, eat food as really offered to an idol."

In some cases a difference of translation does not reflect a better manuscript evidence, that is to say, it does not mean that some earlier manuscript has been found which has a more correct wording, but we see more clearly now what is the meaning of the original. In Romans 1:17 we are accustomed to finding the words, "The just shall live by faith." This declaration has been a clarion call to faith and has been the text for many a sermon on the necessity of continued faith throughout life. It is true that this verse may have this meaning, but it is more probable that it means, "He who through faith is righteous shall live." This is in keeping with the whole emphasis of Paul throughout Romans, which has as its theme "justification by faith" (Romans 5:1). Paul does not present two themes in Romans: the one "living by faith" and the other "justification by faith." His purpose was to emphasize one great primary truth of Christian doctrine: the righteousness which comes by faith in God. It is a kind of imputed righteousness, which has its origin in the grace of God and its response in the faith of man. Not only is this translation more in keeping with the Pauline context, but it is more faithful to the Hebrew of Habakkuk 2:4, of which it is a quotation.

For the average laymen and for some theological students, Greek is regarded as "quite impossible" and Hebrew is simply "for another world." For the Bible translator who wishes to do his work well, they become a daily necessity, which constantly enhance the value and effectiveness of the translation and reward the translator with some of his most priceless spiritual experiences.

CHAPTER 5

FROM THE DAYS
OF PENTECOST

Translating the words of life into the mother tongue of countless thousands is no new adventure in faith or sudden departure from the plan of God in the proclamation of the Good News. In fact, "Each Man in His Own Language" was the startling news in Jerusalem over nineteen hundred years ago. Throngs of Jews and proselytes had come from Parthia and Media in the east, from Phrygia and Pamphylia to the north, from Egypt and Libya in the south, from Crete and Rome in the west. There were merchants, bankers, ship captains, and pilgrims all crowded into Jerusalem for the holy ceremonies of spring, drawn to the ancient "City of Peace"; some desirous of worshiping in the temple, others wanting renewed friendships, and many bent on making profitable business deals. For the most part the Greek language served this motley throng, and for those who might not know Greek, there were always bilingual Aramaic speakers to serve as go-betweens. But scarcely had the Holy Spirit fallen upon the huddled band of anxious waiting disciples, when the startling news of their witness ran like wildfire through multitudes: "Have you heard those Galileans? They are speaking in our own languages. Listen to them!" Fear and wonder gripped the hearts of the crowd which listened to Peter proclaim the prophecy of Joel and the promises of David. On that very day some three thousand persons repented and were baptized, for they had heard the message of salvation proclaimed to them in a language which spoke with clarity and power, for it was in the language of their souls—their mother tongue.

The miracle of Pentecost pointed the way for the early church. The message of life was to be proclaimed in living words. It was not strange that the New Testament was written in the Koiné Greek, the language of the man in the street. The Gospel writers did not seek out the professors of rhetoric in order to have their simple language embellished with high-sounding metaphors and academic phrases. The beauty of what they wrote was not in the ornateness of the language, but in the sublimity of their thoughts. Without doubt many of the followers of Jesus wrote down their recollections of what He had said to them, and they must have frequently used Aramaic, which was the language of Palestine, known by peasants and nobles alike. But the message of the Gospels was for the world, not just Palestine, and hence it was to be expected that the Gospel accounts would be written in Greek, even though they may have drawn heavily upon some of the Aramaic sources and though the wording often seems to reflect the Aramaic form in which Jesus may have spoken to the people. The Koiné Greek was the second language of Palestine, and the language of all the Eastern half of the Roman Empire. It was the fitting vehicle for a message written to the then known world.

The plot of the Jewish leaders to stamp out a local heresy was partially responsible for its becoming a world religion. They scattered the Christians, but in so doing they only multiplied the churches. As a result they had to send a young man named Saul as far away as Damascus to try to eradicate what they regarded as this plague in Judaism. But wherever men went they carried a message of repentance, forgiveness, and a new way of life. It is impossible to know into which language this message was first translated and formally written down. But possibly the first circulated translations were in Syriac, the language of the Judean Christians' northern neighbors. Many believe that Tatian compiled his story of the Gospels sometime in the second century. Certainly Tatian had a missionary task in mind. He wove from the four Gospel accounts a continuous story of the Life of Christ. To his work has been given the name of "Diatessaron," meaning literally, "According to the Four." This was an introduction to the life of Jesus for the Syriac-speaking Christians, but soon they had the entire New Testament, called the Peshito Version, meaning "The Simple Version." Here again, the translators sought to render the words of life by the vocabulary of living men and women. This was the Syriac translation which provided the Bibles for the Nestorian Christians, who became the great missionaries to the East, where they spread from Persia, into Arabia, India, Turkestan, and China. Their churches in China died out, at least in some measure because they failed to carry on the heritage which was theirs in the Syriac, for they did not make the Scriptures available to their Chinese neighbors. In South India they continued as the Church of St. Thomas, where even until now many of the ministers of the churches read the Scriptures in Syriac and then translate verbally in Malayalam.

Friendly neighbors were not the only peoples who received the Message of Life. Bitter enemies of the ancient Greco-Roman world also received the Word, and from the least likely source. Tradition records the destructive raids of the seagoing Visigoths upon the mainland of Greece and Asia Minor. These hordes of Teutonic warriors were not content with the booty of gold, silver, iron, silks, linen, and spices. They dragged away the plundered inhabitants and made them their slaves. But among these unfortunate victims of the marauding Goths were some earnest Christians, who in humble faith and self-evident holiness brought the light of the gospel message to their warring captors.

Those whom Rome could not fully conquer she often attempted to assimilate, and so after a costly defeat inflicted upon the Goths, in A.D. 332, the Roman legions were opened to divisions of Gothic soldiers, sworn to defend the Roman Empire. However, their position was probably rather similar to that of well-treated hostages.

Serving among some of these Gothic troops as a kind of chaplain was a man called Ulfilas. He was officially known as a "reader" of the Scriptures to the troops, and it may have been during his service with these Gothic warriors stationed near Constantinople that Ulfilas first realized the need of translating the Word of God into the Germanic tongue of his companions-in-arms.

Ulfilas' ability as a preacher, his knowledge of Greek, Latin, and Gothic, and his administrative gifts came to the attention of the church leaders of the area. Soon Eusebius appointed this comparatively young man as Bishop of Gothia. The title was, however, more imposing than his churches, for his task was primarily a missionary one. He had to preach, baptize, and organize his bishopric against the opposition of an irascible and irreligious king. For seven years Ulfilas labored north of the Danube trying to encourage his little flock and win the hearing of men who were more interested in war than in worship. Finally, the Gothic warlords would have no more of this preacher and expelled both him and his followers from the land. By petition to Emperor Constantius the Bishop to the Goths sought refuge for his little flock within the borders of the Roman Empire and at last was able to bring them across the Danube to settle near the present-day Plevna, thus earning for himself the title of "Moses of the Goths." It is uncertain how much Ulfilas was able to return to the regions beyond the Danube in order to carry on his evangelistic work, nor do we know just the degree to which the theological controversies of his day consumed his time and energies, but the one enduring task for which Ulfilas has been justly praised is his translation of the Bible into Gothic. Some ancient writers even give him the credit of having invented the Gothic alphabet. Undoubtedly he refined it and made numerous improvements on it, but it is probable that others before him had made some adaptations of the Greek and Roman alphabets in order to write the strange sounds in which Gothic seemed to abound. But there was little consistency in usage, a fact which is reflected in the numerous ways in which Ulfilas' name has been written by his contemporaries: *Vulfila,*

Gulfila, Ulfila, Oulphilas, Ourphilas, and *Wulfila,* all of which are transliterations of the Gothic name meaning "Little Wolf." Similar difficulties existed in transliterating Greek borrowings into Gothic. Some of these inconsistencies give us important clues as to the pronunciation of the respective languages at the time.

A good deal of Ulfilas' New Testament has been preserved for us in the famous Silver Codex and some fragments of his Old Testament are known from secondary sources. To his translation we owe a debt of gratitude, not only for its important missionary ministry but also for its wealth of information about the roots of our own Germanic tongue, English.

Whether Ulfilas was able to complete the entire Bible before his death, sometime around A.D. 383, we do not know, but we learn that some twenty years later some of his own translation helpers were in correspondence with the world-famous scholar Jerome, who was translating the Scriptures into Latin in his cloistered rooms in a monastery in Bethlehem. These Gothic translators wanted more information about some of the difficult texts of the Bible, and what was more natural than for one Bible translator to get in touch with another, for their problems then, even as now, were much the same.

It was not enough for the early Christians to give the Scriptures to their neighbors, such as the Syrians, the Copts of Egypt, and the Ethiopians, and to their enemies, the Goths; they gave the Word also to their rulers, the Romans. We have no idea of those who first translated the Scriptures into Latin, but we do know that there were many, for Augustine complained in his day of "an abundance of interpreters." To the most widely circulated form of these early Latin translations was given the name of Itala, but these included many inconsistencies of text and rendering, so that it is scarcely any wonder that in A.D. 382 Pope Damasus of Rome was quick to see in the brilliant young monk Eusebius Sophronius Hieronymus someone who might bring order out of chaos and produce a Latin translation which would be understood by all.

Jerome, for he is thus known to posterity, had formerly been in Rome to study rhetoric and philosophy, but there the claims of Christ had laid hold of him and he was baptized. Rather than settling down to his profession an internal restlessness drove him to travel. First, he journeyed to Gaul and then to Asia Minor. Finally, he joined a band of ascetic desert dwellers in the wilderness of Chalcis, where he studied the Scriptures intensively. After a brief stay in Constantinople he was back in Rome, browned by the desert sun, clothed in the harsh garments of an ascetic, and preaching stirring messages to the dilettantes of patrician heritage, a number of whom he convinced to abandon their lives of aimless artificiality. Two women of this number dedicated their Aventine palace as an asylum for the poor.

Having served Pope Damasus efficiently as a secretary for one of the church gatherings in Rome, Jerome was soon at work on the task of revising the New Testament, which was completed in about three years. His task was no easy one, for people had become attached to the wording of the Itala. To change it was regarded by some as pure blasphemy. Jerome tried to describe his plight by saying:

If my occupation had been to plait rush baskets or to weave mats out of palm leaves, in order, by the sweat of my brow, to gain my daily bread, envy would have spared me. But since in obedience to the precepts of the Saviour, I have, for the good of souls, chosen to prepare the bread which perishes not and have wished to clear the path of truth of the weeds which ignorance has sown in it, I am accused of a two-fold crime. If I correct errors in the Sacred Text, I am denounced as a falsifier; if I do not correct them, I am pilloried as a disseminator of error.

One only wishes, however, that Jerome had felt more at liberty to correct some of the glaring inconsistencies that the Itala tradition had bequeathed the church. The same Greek words were often translated by quite different Latin terms, and without rhyme or reason. For instance, the Greek *archiereus* "chief priest" is sometimes rendered as *princeps sacerdotum*, other times as *summus sacerdos*, and in still other places as *pontifex*. Little did Jerome realize that his inconsistencies would be a problem to a revision committee preparing a Spanish Version in the twentieth century. Jerome's discrepancies were inherited by the early Spanish translators, who then passed them on, so that many Spanish people assume that the three equivalent Spanish expressions *príncipe de los sacerdotes, sumo sacerdote,* and *pontífice* refer to three different offices, rather than being translations of one and the same original Greek term.

Jerome might have continued his work at Rome had not the death of Damasus and the jealousy of the new pope made it imperative for him to seek some refuge in a less conspicuous part of the Empire. By this time, however, Jerome was desirous of mastering Hebrew, even as he understood Greek. And what better place to do that than in Palestine? Soon, he was setting out for the Holy Land, surrounded by some of his loyal converts, who joined him in establishing in Bethlehem a church, houses for his comrades in the faith, and a hospice to shelter the hordes of pilgrims who visited the place of Jesus' birth.

For thirty-four years Jerome continued in Bethlehem and for the most part worked at the task of translating the Old Testament from Hebrew into Latin, but he also found time to write twenty-four books of Bible commentaries, two church histories, some biographies of Christian hermits, and a number of treatises on church affairs and doctrinal problems.

Some twenty years were devoted to the consuming task of translating the Old Testament into Latin. And not until A.D. 405, when Jerome was sixty-five, was the work completed. Toward the end his eyesight failed, and others had to read to him the Hebrew scrolls while he dictated the translation. His publication of the books of Samuel and Kings brought a storm of disapproval from some of the bishops in the West, who accused him of promoting his personal interpretations by means of his translation. Even when the entire Old Testament was finished the opposition was by no means quieted. Jerome could see, however, that despite the denunciations of jealous churchmen his translation would win out in the end, for, as he wrote, "They attack it in public and read it in secret."

More and more both clergy and laity began to read this masterful translation prepared for the people as a whole, from which fact it gained the name of *vulgatus*, and is known today as the Vulgate. It was universally honored by the church in the West and became the official translation. Whenever a council of the church convened, the Vulgate was carried in triumph in a golden reliquary. The tragedy was that the church began more and more to leave the Bible in a golden reliquary, for as the church became concerned with the problem of authority all other issues took second place. The church succeeded in establishing its authority over the disintegrating society of early medieval times, but by exerting its authority over the secular life it lost its own soul. Its message became shrouded from the people and the clergy alike, and even those who honored the Vulgate forgot the meaning of its divine proclamation of redemption.

CHAPTER 6

BOUND BY THE
HOLY SCRIPTURES

Charles V, Emperor of the Holy Roman Empire, sat with his council of clerics and state officials to accept the admission of heresy from a troublesome monk, whose fiery preaching had inflamed a thousand torches of revolt against the church and state. At first the Roman Church had refused to pay much attention, for there had been other reformers whose heretical views had been successfully stamped out, but here was a man of stubborn will and keen mind, of thorough training and profound knowledge, a man who had identified himself with the Word of God as opposed to the edicts of the church. In the face of excommunication and threatened death, his words rang out to the assembled throng of defiant enemies and a few valiant friends, "I am bound by the Holy Scriptures."

These words of Luther reflect both the compulsion and the inspiration of the Reformation. The knowledge of the Bible was the motivating force which stirred the lives of millions, for whom the church had been the only known mediator of divine salvation. The living Christ was unshackled from ecclesiastical bondage and the message of life became life and liberty for spiritually enslaved peoples.

But Luther was not the first one to challenge the authority of the church and to be bound by the Holy Scriptures. Waldo, a businessman in Lyons, France, in about A.D. 1170 became intensely curious as to the content of the Scriptures. But he could not read Latin, and so the Scriptures were a closed book to him. However, he hired two money-minded priests, who, in violation of strict regulations, translated the Bible for him into Provençal, the language of southern France. The content of the Word of God made such an impression upon this earnest man that he gave up his business, took upon himself a vow of poverty, and dedicated himself to the simple preaching of the contents of God's Word. In 1179 Rome was willing to grant him a confirmation of his vow to poverty but refused to permit him to preach, for "What truth could a man preach who did not know Latin?" was the watchcry of the ecclesiastical authorities.

The Latin of the church only mystified its hearers and Waldo's humble preaching edified the souls of men. His words were not spectacular but powerful, as he pleaded with them to repent. Much of his preaching and that of his followers consisted in reciting long passages of Scripture in the vernacular. Many of them could not afford an expensive handwritten copy of the Bible, and the ecclesiastical authorities could too easily rob them of such a book, but they could not erase the words which were treasured in the heart. These humble preachers insisted that alms and masses were of no avail for the dead, that purgatory was not Scriptural, that episcopal indulgences were invalid, that prayer was of more value in the secrecy of the closet than in the pomp of the church, and that forgiveness was to be found in a humble and contrite heart and not in ecclesiastical pronouncements.

It is little wonder that such a message won loyal disciples and provoked intense opposition. By 1194 Alfonzo II of Spain threatened with confiscation and persecution anyone who gave food or drink to a follower of Waldo or even listened to anything said by one of these outlawed preachers. In A.D. 1211 eighty Waldensians were burned to death in Strassburg for refusing to recant. But the message of the Bible spread on into Germany, France, Bohemia, Hungary, and Poland. The preaching had to be in secret and the messengers of the Good News often disguised themselves as carpenters, merchants, blacksmiths, or tailors. Wherever they could find a hearing, they left a message of hope and faith with these "friends," for this was the name employed among themselves to identify those who had welcomed the truth of God. The Inquisition relentlessly sought out these "friends" and destroyed them, so that in some places their witness was almost entirely destroyed, but the seeds of the truth were planted where they brought forth fruit in the courageous ministry of the vilified Wyclif.

"Doctor Wicked-Believer," "Flatteries Sinke," "Lying Glutton," "Devells Instrument" was thought to be dying. The ecclesiastical authorities of England rejoiced, for at last they thought they would be rid of this blight on the church. But John Wyclif did not die until 1384, six years later, during which time he continued his attacks upon ecclesiastical corruption and pressed forward in his earnest desire that all men in England might have the knowledge of the Scriptures in their mother tongue. The hierarchy continued their bitter hatred of Wyclif even after his death. Twenty-four years later they attempted to stamp out everything that Wyclif had written, including his translation of the Bible. But the ministry of this man Wyclif continued to haunt them. Even forty-four years after his death they dug up his bones, burned them and threw them into the Swift, a stream near his home in Lutterworth, so that the remains of such a man might not seem to desecrate the hallowed soil of England.

Wyclif's convictions were born out of the desperate times in which he lived and as a result of his teaching theology. The church in England had leagued itself with certain of the aristocracy in order to enslave the masses. Preaching consisted in anecdotes about the lives of the saints, while churchmen insisted that they were the only ones who could tell the people what they ought to think. The more Wyclif lectured on theology at Oxford University the more convinced he became that changes must be made. He was convinced that this transformation which England so terribly needed could not come about unless the people had the Scriptures in their own language, for up till then they were known only in Latin, and relatively few of even the clergymen possessed a copy.

Wyclif's popularity at the University won him the loyal following of such men as John Purvey and Nicholas de Hereford, who helped him with his translation, and Lord Cobham, who financed its publication. But publication was not enough, for most of the people could not read and in those days before the printing press it was impossible to make enough cheap, handwritten copies for wide distribution. Accordingly, Wyclif formed a group called "the Poor Priests." These men traveled from door to door across England, reading the Scriptures, reciting long passages from memory, exhorting the people to repentance and a new life. These humble servants of God, dressed in homespun garments and sandals, often carrying a Bible hidden in their long coarse robes to prevent detection by the ever-watchful authorities, were a severe contrast to the elegant splendor of the landed clergy.

John Purvey reflected the spirit of this devout band of Bible-loving men in his description of what a true translator should be:

A translatour hath nede to lyve a clene lif, and be ful devout in preiers, and have not his wit ocupied about worldli thingis, that the Holi Spiryt, autour of wisdom and kunnyng and truthe, dresse him in his werk and suffre him not for to erre. By this maner, and with good lyving and greet travel, men moun come to trewe and cleer translating, and a trewe undurstonding of Holi Writ, seme it nevere so hard at the bigynnyng. God graunte to us alle grace to kunne wel and kepe wel Holi Writ, and suffre ioiefulli sum peyne for it at laste.

The Poor Priests, also called Lollards, gained so much popularity that the king and the church could not let them go unchallenged. Hence, there began a reign of terror for these sincere men, who were imprisoned, burned at the stake, and harried out of the land. Lord Cobham paid for his part in the Lollard movement by being burned to death, but a few escaped and found refuge in Bohemia, where a man who had read the writings of Wyclif had lighted the fires of religious revolt.

John Huss was a poor student at the University of Prague when he read some of the inflammatory literature written by a man called John Wyclif, professor of theology at Oxford. Huss' soul was thrilled with the realism and the truth of these attacks upon those theological dogmas which were only the tradition of the church and not the teachings of Scripture. By 1405 Huss was a powerful synodical preacher, but his popularity made him dangerous to officialdom, which was suspicious of his transported Lollardism. Huss was deposed, but soon entered the controversy involving the University of Prague. Huss had learned Wyclif's arguments well, and he used them with such force and clarity that he succeeded in making the University a national school.

There was no need for Huss to follow Wyclif in the matter of Bible translating, for he had the entire Bible in the Czech language. But Huss is associated with the Czech Bible because he and his followers undertook a thorough revision of it. It was inevitable that Huss should have turned to the Bible and sought constantly to refine its form and publish its contents, for the Bible was his authority in combating the tenets of his opponents, who insisted that the church consisted solely of the pope as its head and the cardinals as its body. For Huss it was unthinkable that anyone but Christ could be the head and the believers the body.

Huss' heresy, which insisted upon the authority of Scripture, could not be countenanced and so he was indicted by ecclesiastical courts. Though he was guaranteed safe conduct to and during his trial, he was seized, chained, and thrown into a dungeon. When threatened with death if he did not recant, he only declared, "I wish for nothing but to be convinced from Holy Scripture." Then in the presence of his judges, who had already determined sentence against him, he fell upon his knees; but instead of begging for mercy, he lifted his voice in prayer to God to forgive all his enemies. This was too much, and so his priestly robes and ornaments were torn from him, and a high paper hat was put upon his head, on which was written "Heretic." He was then led off to his death.

While chained to the stake, with wood and straw piled up to his neck, he was given one last chance to recant, but sternly refused with the words, "God is my witness that I have never taught that of which I have been accused by false witnesses. In the truth of the Gospel which I have written, taught, and preached, I will die today with gladness." Then as the flames surged around him, he sang with uplifted voice, "Christ, thou Son of the Living God, have mercy upon me."

Huss, who had sung for bread as a poor student of the University of Prague, proclaimed in 1415 a message in the midst of the flames, which would be heard by another poor student in Germany almost a century later.

"I am bound by the Holy Scriptures. My conscience is captive to the Word of God. Unless I am convinced by Scripture or by clear argument, I cannot and will not recant." Luther was never convinced and did not recant, but the storm of ecclesiastical opposition made it necessary for him to go into hiding at Wartburg Castle under the assumed name of Junker Georg. But here he undertook his most important work, translating the New Testament into German, a task which was completed in about one year and first printed in September, 1522.

Luther had been brought up in a strict religious atmosphere in which he had come to be terrified by the wrath of God in punishment for sin. His schooling at the University of Erfurt was designed to prepare him to be a lawyer, but this did not satisfy the needs of young Martin's soul. He resolved to become a monk and on July 17, 1505, entered the Augustinian monastery at Erfurt, and in 1507 was ordained to the priesthood. Still his theological studies brought him no inward peace. He continued to study and in 1512 received the doctorate of theology, but even that and a pilgrimage to Rome did not satisfy the longing heart of a man who wanted to know God. It was at this time that Luther's attention shifted from philosophically argued theology to Biblically proclaimed reality.

Luther found his answer in Paul's proclamation of "justification by faith." What mattered more than the authority of the church was the obedience to Christ as revealed in Scripture.

When Johann Tetzel came to Wittenberg in 1517 selling indulgences, by which the church authorities became rich through promising forgiveness from sins in exchange for money, Luther determined to take action and did so by nailing ninety-five theses to the door of the castle church at Wittenberg. But within two weeks these theses had spread throughout Germany, gaining for Luther an unexpected fame. Luther's sympathizers hailed his pronouncements with joy, and his enemies determined to egg him on so that they might convict him of heresy and destroy his popularity. Within a short time Luther launched an attack against the abuses of the poor by the church. He denied the Scriptural validity of the pope's power, attacked the Roman view of the Lord's Supper (which contended that the bread and wine became the actual body of Jesus), and pressed for reforms, including the reduction of ecclesiastical levies and taxes, the curbing of misdemeanors by the mendicant orders, the suppression of luxury among the clergy, and the recognition of secular government.

It is no wonder that Luther was indicted for all this and brought to trial by the Diet of Worms on April 16, 1521. But his opponents could not secure his confession of guilt nor his recantation; and though they forced him into hiding for a time, they did not still his voice or stop the intense activity of his pen.

The impact of Luther's preaching and the publication of his New Testament in the language of the people stirred such a movement among the people that civil revolt and revolution broke out. Luther was fearful of such chaotic upheavals which seemed to threaten the very existence of society, and as a result he urged the merciless suppression of the Peasants' War, but did not at the same time forget to plead for mercy after the victory. It is difficult for us to judge Luther's action in opposing those who had so wholeheartedly accepted his teachings, even going beyond what he had implied.

But whether we approve or disapprove, we must admit that Luther attempted to deal with this problem in the light of Scripture as he interpreted it.

Luther resumed his teaching at Wittenberg and surprised his friends and foes by marrying. During this time he began his translation of the Old Testament, a task which was to occupy his devotion and energy for eleven years. Not until 1534 was the entire Bible translated and published in German.

Luther was insistent that his translations should "sing the Lord's song in a strange land." To do this was no easy task, for there are so many things in the Bible which were not known in the Germany of Luther's day. Luther was not content to pass over hard words and difficult phrases by simply transliterating them into German. He knew that they would mean no more than they would in Hebrew letters, except that the German alphabet might make them appear more deceptively familiar. He sought out Jewish scholars to gain information about Old Testament weights and measures. He visited slaughterhouses to get the terms which could be used to describe various processes and objects of Old Testament sacrifice. He studied the court jewels in order to make certain that he had the proper names for the gems of the book of Revelation. He listened to children in their play and to artisans in their work. From all of them he gleaned a rich harvest of words to be used in the translation of the Bible, which he insisted should be in the language of the people and not in the pedantic, high-sounding German of the university classroom and the law courts.

Luther's translation became the cornerstone of the new Protestant faith—"protestant," from the original meaning of this word, namely, "to witness," for these men witnessed to the redeeming grace of God in Christ. This witness spurred an Englishman, William Tyndale, to do for his native land what Luther was doing for his.

The Bishop of London was frantic. More and more New Testaments published in Europe by the harassed William Tyndale were being smuggled into England and spreading the flames of church revolt. Bishop Tunstall set out to find this Englishman who had fled to the Continent in order to defy the laws of the land and who in 1525 had published the Scriptures in the English tongue.

Bishop Tunstall tried to stamp out the heresy of Bible reading in England. To do this he had ordered homes invaded and Testaments seized. Those who possessed them were arrested as heretics. He also went to the Continent to track down this disseminator of lies but could not discover his refuge. However, he did meet a merchant Augustine Packington, who pretended to serve the bishop's interests and promised to procure for him a sizable quantity of these contraband books, though he warned him that the price would not be low.

Packington went immediately to his friend Tyndale and explained his deal with the Bishop of London. Promptly the bishop was offered the rest of an entire edition, one in which Tyndale had already discovered some renderings which he wanted to improve. With the handsome price which the bishop was only too glad to pay, Tyndale was able to put out an entire new and corrected edition.

With his hundreds of Testaments Bishop Tunstall returned in triumph to London, where with Cardinal Wolsey he staged the famous burning at Paul's Cross in London. There he piled one hundred and fifty-eight baskets of Tyndale's Testaments, and the heretics, who were arrested for having possessed a copy, were forced to throw burning fagots on the books.

The bishop had his fire, but all of England soon had more and better New Testaments.

William Tyndale was well prepared for his task of translating the Bible, for he had spent almost twenty years in the universities of Oxford and Cambridge, probably transferring to the latter school in order to attend the lectures of the famous Erasmus, who lectured on Greek at Cambridge from 1509 to 1514. It was at Cambridge that he also met John Frith, who was to prove his loyal friend and helper. Tyndale then went to live with Sir John Walsh, a knight of Gloucestershire, as a tutor for his children. But he soon stirred up bitter resentment among the prelates who enjoyed the hospitality of the Walsh manor and found themselves embarrassed by the unanswerable arguments of this man who kept quoting the Scriptures and insisted on the simplicity of true faith through Christian living and Bible reading.

Tyndale had by this time determined to translate the Bible into the English of his day, for such vast changes had occurred in the speech of Englishmen since the days of Wyclif that the former translation was no longer usable. But to translate the Scriptures into English he had to obtain the permission of Bishop Tunstall of London, who was in no mood to grant any such right to a suspected priest like William Tyndale, particularly since Tyndale had been publicly threatened and reviled by Chancellor Parker, supervisor of all priests within the Gloucestershire diocese.

Tyndale went on to London where he preached in a poor parish of St. Dunstans-in-the-West. His earnest message attracted the attention of a wealthy cloth merchant Sir Humphrey Monmouth, who took Tyndale into his home so that he could carry on the task to which he wished to dedicate himself completely. England, however, was no place for a man to undertake such a revolutionary project, and so with money lent to him by Sir Humphrey, Tyndale set out to the Continent. He is reported to have gone first to Hamburg and in Germany he may have had contact with Luther, but for this period of self-imposed obscurity there are few records and only scant tradition. After about a year of exile, Tyndale was ready with his "New Testament in simplest language, and in the vulgar tongue," but he had to go to Cologne to find a printer who would be willing to print such forbidden literature.

Despite all possible precautions news of this undertaking reached the ears of Cochlaeus, who was famous for his anti-Protestant atrocities. First, he warned Cardinal Wolsey and Bishop Tunstall in England and then proceeded with vengeance against Tyndale. But before he could raid the print shop and destroy the work, Tyndale learned of the plot and escaped to Worms, Germany, taking with him his precious manuscript and the completed pages of the first twenty-two chapters of Matthew. Soon the books were ready and by the spring of 1526 at least six thousand copies had been smuggled into England.

Bishop Tunstall tried desperately to stamp out this smuggling, but all his efforts were fruitless. The burning of the New Testaments only heightened the demand so that certain Dutch printers put out editions quite independently of Tyndale. Frustrated in his efforts to seize Tyndale, the Bishop of London turned against Tyndale's former friends. Many were excommunicated, others imprisoned, and some burned at the stake. Even Sir Humphrey Monmouth was not spared.

Tyndale then set himself to translate the Old Testament and pushed forward in his task with feverish haste, but he had not completed Chronicles when in 1535 ecclesiastical agents arrested him by guile and imprisoned him in Vilvorde Castle not far from Antwerp. His trial dragged on for sixteen months, during which time he surreptitiously continued his translation with the aid of his jailor, whom he had led to Jesus Christ. Finally his death sentence was passed and he was strangled in the prison courtyard, after which his body was burned at the stake. His last words were reported as "Lord open the King of England's eyes."

His prayer was not long in fulfillment for that very year his own translation was published in England. The revolt of Henry VIII against the papacy resulted in the execution of Bishop Tunstall for treason, and the open licensing of Scripture publication; so that even during the protracted trial of Tyndale, Miles Coverdale, who had worked with Tyndale some years before in Hamburg, published his complete Bible, based very largely upon Tyndale's heroic work.

Other English versions followed: the Matthew Bible (1537), which was a combination of the work of Tyndale and Coverdale; the Great Bible (1539), published by Cromwell; the Geneva Bible (1560); and the Bishops' Bible (1568). In all of these the work of Tyndale and Coverdale figures most prominently. When in 1604

King James appointed a commission to prepare still another version which would be acceptable to Puritans and Anglicans alike, it is not strange that the forty-seven scholars found in the versions of Tyndale and Coverdale so much of the wording which has now become familiar to us in the so-called King James Version, published in 1611.

CHAPTER 7

INTO ALL THE WORLD

The dynamic story of the Reformation and the Bible cannot be told simply in terms of English, German, and Czech (Bohemian). The torch of truth lighted the page of Holy Writ in numerous vernaculars and by the end of the sixteenth century whole Bibles had been published in Italian (1471), Catalan (1478), Dutch (1522), French (1530), Swedish (1541), Danish (1550), Spanish (1553), Polish (1561), Slavonic (1581), Icelandic (1584), Slovenian (1584), Welsh (1588), and Hungarian (1590). During the following two centuries Scriptures were published in forty-nine other languages. Among these was an entire Bible for the Massachusetts Indians.

John Eliot, the Cambridge-trained pastor of the small Puritan parish of Roxbury, arrived in the Massachusetts Bay Colony just eleven years after the first pilgrims, but the memory of John Robinson's rebuke to the *Mayflower* passengers rang within his heart, ". . . concerning the killing of those poor Indians. Oh! how happy a thing had it been, if you had converted some. . . ." Fifteen years after his first contact with these Algonkian people, he was preaching at Nonantum in the Great Wigwam of Waban, chief of the Massachusetts Indians of that region. His teacher had been Job Nesutan, a brilliant young Indian who had learned English and who came to live in the Eliot household in order to teach his host the strange sounds and the even stranger grammar—nothing even slightly resembling the Hebrew and Greek which Eliot had studied at Cambridge. John Eliot also spent long periods with these Algonkian braves, and there he mastered their vocabulary and learned to understand their manner of life. Among them he learned the word *mugwump*, which he used to translate "duke" in Genesis 36:30, making the verse read: "Mugwump Dishon, Mugwump Ezer, Mugwump Dishan. . . ." By 1663 the entire Bible was published, the first Bible published in the Western Hemisphere. But within fifty years of Eliot's death the tribe was practically extinct. Wars, disease, and relentless pressure from Whites resulted in the extinction of a tribe.

It was not until the nineteenth century—"the Missionary Century"—that translations began to appear in great numbers, but within a single century Scriptures had been published in 494 languages and dialects, nor has the pace slackened in the twentieth century. In many of these 494 languages only a few books were published, but a number received New Testaments, and some obtained Bibles. Of those languages which received less than a Testament in the nineteenth century, more than 100 had New Testaments or Bibles printed during the first half of the twentieth century.

The great missionary century saw missionaries pioneering in almost every part of the globe, and translations came forth in such languages as Persian, Bengali, Burmese, Kalmuk Mongolian, Assamese, Malay, Chinese, Japanese, Korean, Cherokee (U. S. A.), Aztec, Miskito (Nicaragua), Arawak (British and Dutch), Yoruba (West Africa), Herero (South Africa), Swahili (East Africa), Bulu (Central Africa), Batta (Sumatra), Gilbertese (Gilbert Islands), Kusaien (Caroline Islands), Rarotonga (Cook Islands), Malagasy (Madagascar). To understand this momentous time in the history of evangelism we must catch some glimpses of how certain of these translations came about.

Adoniram Judson was a discouraged man. Six years had passed since he had begun work in Burma in 1813, after trying to enter India, only to be refused permission by the East India Company. For six long years Judson had labored incessantly on the language, had tried to preach to the people, and had read his faltering translations, but there was almost no response. The government opposition to his work had grown alarmingly so that he feared that his three timid converts would be discovered and tortured to death. Added to all this had been the death of his first child and his wife's failing health.

Judson determined to visit the King of Burma in the sumptuous palace at Ava, but his personally presented petition was of no avail. He had thought of abandoning the work when the persistent requests and pleas of his Burmese converts led him to remain and to dedicate himself afresh to evangelism and especially to the study of the language and translating. Of his trials with the language he wrote:

> When we find the letters and words all totally destitute of the least resemblance to any language we have ever met with, and these words not clearly divided and distinguished as in Western writing, by breaks and points and capitals, but run together in one continuous line, a sentence or paragraph seeming to the eye but one long word; when, instead of separate characters on paper, we find only obscure scratches on dried palm leaves strung together and called a book; when we have no dictionary and no interpreter to explain a single word and must get something of the language before we can avail ourselves of the assistance of a native teacher—that is work!

Not long after this, Judson and his colleague Dr. Jonathan Price were summoned to the royal court: Judson to act as interpreter and Dr. Price to be court physician. However, England and Burma were soon at war and that meant imprisonment for all white foreigners.

For eleven long months Judson lay bound in heavy chains and fetters in a vermin-infested jail, bitten by swarms of mosquitoes and flies, suffering immeasurably from the intense heat and the stifling humidity. Without the help brought by his brave wife he would certainly have died. However, his principal concern seemed to be for the manuscript on which he had been working. It was no longer safe in their mission home, for that had been raided. To preserve those precious pages, Mrs. Judson sewed them into a pillow and Adoniram slept on it for the rest of the agonizing time spent in the prison Let-ma-yoon-taung. Finally Judson was unbound from his fetters, only to be chained to a long line of slowly dying men, who were to begin the death march to the dungeons of Oung-pen-la to await execution. Despite Judson's feverish pleas, his pillow was taken from him and cast away as he marched off to apparent total defeat.

After seven more cruel months, Judson was suddenly released to serve as an interpreter under guard. But in a short time, the British defeated the Burmese, and Judson was a free man again, joyfully greeted by his wife, colleagues, and faithful followers. Maung Ing, one of his first three converts, came to greet his "teacher," carrying the old faded pillow, the only one of Judson's possessions which he had been able to rescue on that tragic day at Let-ma-yoon-taung. But there within the tattered cloth were the precious manuscripts. Soon Judson was back at his task of committing to written form the Word of God in the Burmese language. The last page of his translation went to press on December 29, 1835, but for five more years he worked intensely on the revision.

While speaking to a group of Christians in the United States concerning the almost insurmountable difficulties of bringing the gospel to Oriental lands, he was asked whether the prospects were bright for the conversion of the world; to which this man of God, who had known bitter suffering, keen disappointment, and endless toil, declared with assurance, "As bright, Sir, as the promises of God."

The promises of God had been the strength of his life and the heart of his message.

Robert Morrison was a strange spectacle. Dressed in Chinese coat and thick shoes, wearing his hair in a pigtail down his back, Morrison lived alone in an abandoned French warehouse between the massive walls of Canton and the Pearl River. Official decrees made ordinary missionary work next to impossible, for the Chinese law declared in substance:

From this time forward, such Europeans as shall privately print books and establish preachers who shall propagate their religion shall have this to look to: the chief or principal one shall be executed. . . .

Morrison could not openly hire teachers to assist him with the language. But at last he obtained the help of two Chinese scholars who taught him at the risk of their lives, for apprehension meant sure death by slow torture. One of his teachers was in such constant fear of being caught and tortured that he constantly carried a vial of poison to save himself from such a dire fate.

Morrison's fine education and the backing of the London Missionary Society had not been enough to obtain permission from the East India Company in order to sail to Canton. In fact, he had had to go to New York, and only after constant rebuffs and discouraging advice had he prevailed upon one ship captain to hide him aboard and put him ashore one hundred and thirteen days later at Canton, China's only open port in 1807. But Canton was only open for six months each year, after which time Morrison had to go to the Portuguese-held island of Macao.

In order to return to Canton at all, Morrison had to accept a job as translator with the East India Company, where during the day he handled the routine business of trade and prepared an English-Chinese Dictionary and a Chinese Grammar in which the East India Company was much interested. At night he worked with Chinese helpers on a translation of the Bible.

By September of 1809 Morrison had completed the Acts of the Apostles, which he contrived to have published with hand-made wooden blocks. The pages were bound in false covers and distributed free to book dealers, who in turn gladly sold them cheaply at 100 per cent profit. To preserve the wood blocks and to prevent their detection during the yearly season when Morrison had to live in

Macao, he buried them in Canton, only to find upon returning that the termites had devoured them completely.

In spite of trials and delays the New Testament was completed in 1814. Help for this work came from William Milne who had been sent out by the London Missionary Society, but he was not permitted to live in Canton nor even to stay in Macao, but went off to Malacca, from where he still rendered Morrison valuable aid.

The East India Company in China was delighted with Morrison's work and tried to print some of his grammar and dictionary, but the Chinese printers were seized by hostile officials and some of Morrison's manuscripts were carried off together with the type. To make matters worse, some overly enthusiastic supporter of Morrison publicized his achievements so extensively in England that the home office of the East India Company became alarmed and sent a letter to China demanding Morrison's immediate dismissal. But the Canton office could scarcely afford to lose such a valuable man, and so they carried on a protracted correspondence which resulted in his staying on. By 1819 the entire Bible was completed, again with the help of Milne, who translated ten books, and by 1823 Morrison's monumental dictionary of the Chinese language was published by the East India Company.

Morrison, who died in 1834, did not live to see missionary work carried beyond the shadow of Canton's tightly closed walls, but his translation opened the way and prepared the ground for the thousands of dedicated men and women who have followed and have given their lives to take the message of the Word to China's millions. Within a hundred years of Morrison's death Scriptures were distributed in China at the rate of several million each year.

By 1809 the reputation of William Carey and his two colleagues, William Ward and Joshua Marshman, had reached England, but the scholars of Oxford and Cambridge referred cynically to these pioneers in translating the Bible into the languages of India as "low-born and low-bred mechanics." It was true that Carey, an ardent Baptist preacher, did not receive enough from his poor congregations to support himself and earned his living as a shoemaker. But despite his lack of formal training, he had learned Latin, Greek, and Hebrew. Ward was only a printer from Hull, but he had proved to be an ingenious organizer. Marshman had been the master of a charity school at Bristol. Nevertheless, as Robert Southey, poet laureate of England, declared in 1809, "in fourteen years they have done more to spread the knowledge of the Scriptures among the heathen than has been accomplished or even attempted by all the world beside."

William Carey had arrived in India in 1793, but lack of funds, suspicion of villagers, and opposition from the East India Company to any missionary endeavor made it necessary for him to work for that company in order to legalize his presence in the country. On the side, Carey worked assiduously at his translation of the New Testament in Bengali, which was completed in 1799, but the East India Company made it impossible for him to print it.

As there seemed to be no possible help, when William Ward and Joshua Marshman arrived in Calcutta in 1800, the trio, together with their families, established their mission at Serampore, which was then under Danish rule. Marshman and his wife began a school for European children in order to pay the expenses of the mission. Ward began to set up a printing press and taught an Indian blacksmith to cut type from metal, and Carey rewrote and revised his translation, which was published in 1801. Carey's remarkable linguistic gifts were soon recognized by the government and he was given the post of Professor of Bengali in the Government College at Calcutta, a position which he held for thirty years.

Carey soon discovered that many of the languages of India were closely related. His study of Sanskrit opened up the challenge of translating the Scriptures into such derivative languages as Gujarati, Marathi, and Hindi. Carey pleaded for help in the homeland. Among those who responded to these courageous missionary pioneers was the British and Foreign Bible Society, organized on March 7, 1804, in the London Tavern. Their first foreign commitment went to this struggling Serampore translation trio.

Carey and his helpers carried on an amazing program so that by March of 1813 they could report translations published, in manuscript, or in process for ten of the important languages of India. But on the tragic night of March 11 a fire broke out in the print shop and soon three and a half tons of type metal, thousands of pounds of paper, manuscripts of Scripture, grammars, and dictionaries were all destroyed. For faint-hearted men the Serampore mission would have ceased, but not for Carey, Ward, and Marshman, who declared, "We are cast down, but not in despair. . . . Traveling a road a second time is usually done with greater ease and certainty. . . . We shall improve the translations lost."

To such enterprise and faith the Christian world responded with offers to help and within fifty days, people in England raised £10,000 sterling. By the end of the year the printing establishment was rebuilt and operating at twice its earlier capacity.

By the time of Carey's death in 1834 this Serampore trio were responsible for publications in forty-four languages, of which Carey had translated twenty-six, either in whole or in part, either alone or with others. He had lived to see the answer to his life's motto, "Attempt great things for God. Expect great things from God."

One of the manuscripts destroyed in the Serampore fire was the first part of the New Testament in Hindustani, translated by a brilliant young missionary and linguist, Henry Martyn, who had arrived from England in 1806, only seven years before. No one in missionary history has ever equaled the linguistic exploits of Martyn, who in six brief years, during which time his body was often racked with tropical fever and his lungs were gradually being eaten away with incurable tuberculosis, completed translations of the New Testament in Urdu (Hindustani), Persian, and Arabic.

Martyn's preparation for his work had been of the highest order.

He had specialized in Greek and Hebrew at Cambridge, where he graduated at twenty-four years of age, after having won first prize in Latin composition. Martyn had planned to go to the field under the Society for Missions to Africa and the East, but severe financial reverses and the need of supporting his sister led him to go to India as a chaplain to the East India Company's officers and troops.

Martyn's arrival in Calcutta made an indelible impression upon him. The hideous gilded idols, the massive temples, the yellow-robed priests, the pathetic worshipers called by clanging gongs to prayer before grotesque gods seemed to stun Martyn. He wrote home, "I shivered as if standing, as it were, in the neighborhood of hell." But there was hope for India in the missionary activities of Serampore. Marshman and Carey were quick to see what a tremendous asset this young man could be to their work, and they urged him to join them; but Martyn's heart was already turned toward the interior of India and especially the Mohammedan world.

Martyn's preaching in Calcutta was with such fervor and convicting power that when he requested transfer to an interior post at the new station of Patna, the officers in Calcutta seemed glad to grant it. But in Patna Martyn met a motley array of soldiers of fortune. The troops were uninterested and the officers resented any interference from conscientious chaplains. Nevertheless, despite indifference and hostility, Martyn won a major and six soldiers to Christ within a single month.

Except for the time which had to be dedicated to his responsibilities as chaplain, Martyn gave himself to an intensive study of Urdu and was soon so proficient in preaching in the language that he had congregations of more than eight hundred people, which seems incredible considering the strong Mohammedan opposition in the region. Martyn had not been content just with the study of Hindustani, for he insisted on learning the Persian language and studying Arabic. But this had not occupied all of his time, for he also prepared a lovely garden next to his home. He was hoping that a young lady, Lydia Grenfell, would finally consent to join him in India. Month after month he wrote her pleadingly, but at last the important letter arrived. It was "No." On that same day, he was told by the medical officers that he was suffering from an advanced case of tuberculosis.

Rather than destroying his vision and undermining his purpose, these two keen disappointments, a lost sweetheart and lost health, seemed only to spur him on. Soon he was traveling to Persia where he worked with a sense of unparalleled urgency to finish and revise the Persian New Testament, as well as the Arabic. But Martyn was no man to hide away in some room filled with books. He preached so boldly and effectively to the people of Shiraz, where he was living, that a Mohammedan lawyer challenged him to public debate, which was readily accepted. Martyn followed up his verbal encounter with a pamphlet defending the claims of Christ in the light of Moham-medan theology.

Realizing that he could not live very long, Martyn set out on horseback for Constantinople, fifteen hundred miles away, and from there he hoped to take a boat to England. But Martyn did not get further than Tokat, Turkey, where on October 16, 1812, he coughed out his life in a dirty stable, for there was no room in the inn for the sick white traveler.

Henry Martyn had accomplished in six years what few men have accomplished in sixty. He had finished three New Testaments in three different languages: Urdu (published by the Serampore Press, 1814), Persian (published by the Russian Bible Society of St. Peters-burg, 1815), and Arabic (published by the British and Foreign Bible Society, 1816).

"Brother Sherry," as everyone called him, set out in 1867 to walk seven hundred of the nine hundred miles from Peking to Shanghai. He had purchased a discarded Buddhist temple and remodeled it for a Christian chapel, but had turned it over to a colleague, for he had urgent business in Shanghai. A friend had written him about an attractive, brilliant young woman, Susan M. Waring, who had given up a promising literary career to go to China as a missionary-teacher. This was just the woman whom Brother Sherry determined to marry though he had never seen her. Moreover, he did, for in three months he was back in Peking with his charming wife.

Samuel Isaac Joseph Schereschewsky was as determined and swift in learning the Chinese language as he was in romance. Within eighteen months of his arrival in China in 1858 he had acquired an amazing command of Chinese. This was not strange for he already knew Russian, German, English, Greek, and Hebrew.

Schereschewsky was born in Russian Lithuania in 1831 and was educated at the Talmud Torah of Zhitomir, Russia, as well as at the University of Breslau. After arrival in the United States in 1854, a Baptist pastor in New York led this brilliant young Jew to accept Christianity. Soon he was studying theology at a Presbyterian seminary in Pennsylvania (Western Theological Seminary in Alleghany), and in 1858 he entered the Protestant Episcopal Church to be sent as a missionary to China.

Morrison's monumental translation had been in the High Wenli dialect, the literary medium of the scholars. What was needed by the middle of the nineteenth century was a translation into Mandarin, a form of Chinese spoken in the capital city of Peking and in an increasing number of other areas. Schereschewsky was one of seven missionaries commissioned to translate the New Testament, but he was given the entire responsibility for the Old Testament, for which his thorough training in Hebrew had admirably fitted him. By 1873 the entire Bible was completed and published by the American Bible Society.

The mission work was progressing with such rapidity that someone was needed to administer the expanding program, so in 1875 Brother Sherry was made Bishop of Shanghai. One of his first projects was the establishment of a college, the first in China. By 1881 Schereschewsky asked for relief from his many duties as bishop in order that he could translate the Bible into Easy Wenli, a more colloquial form of the language, which would be understood by even more people. But he could not be spared from administrative demands. He attempted to combine both tasks, and as a result of his condition of overwork and chronic fatigue he suffered a crippling attack of paralysis, possibly polio.

Though a prisoner of his wheel chair for twenty-one years, during which time he was totally paralyzed except for the ability to move one hand slightly, nevertheless, he revised his translation of the Mandarin Old Testament, translated the entire Bible into Easy Wenli, completed systems of references for both Bibles, and began a Mongolian dictionary. The Easy Wenli Bible has been called "the One-Finger Bible," for Brother Sherry had to type out the entire translation using just one finger on his typewriter.

Out of the dense green foliage of a tropical Pacific atoll there appeared a dark-skinned native. He was upon the G.I.'s almost before they could whirl and cover him with their rifles. With hands raised and in broken English he cried, "Me Jesus man! Me read God's book!" Then before the astonished soldiers realized it, this man was reading out of a big black book. Here was proof that missionaries had preceded the American troops by many years.

As early as 1819 Hiram Bingham had sailed out of Boston harbor with twelve other missionaries. They began work in Hawaii, but that was only the first steppingstone for evangelistic work to be carried on in scores of Pacific Islands. The enterprising Boston whaling vessels rounded Cape Horn each year and headed out into the Pacific for their catch of whales, but whaling and trade with the Orient also opened up the Pacific Island world to those courageous New England men and women who went to the far-flung outposts of the Pacific to give—not to get.

Hiram Bingham, Jr., after graduation from Yale, followed his father's example and set out for the Gilbert Islands, just to the west of the International Date Line and only a few miles north of the Equator. There he struggled on for five years against serious handicaps of sickness and isolation until he had completed the Gospel of Matthew. The manuscript was sent to the mission printing office in

Honolulu. Bingham watched thirteen long months drag by. At last a boat came bringing cargo from Honolulu, but instead of the Gospels which Bingham was so earnestly expecting, there was a letter explaining that the people in Honolulu were too busy to print the manuscript and so had returned it to him. However, they had sent along a little hand press which he could use in printing the manuscript himself. But he knew nothing of printing, and with so many pressing duties he felt almost too exhausted and sick even to think of having to learn how to do the work himself.

The next morning a lifeboat load of shipwrecked sailors landed on the island. Among them was a man who had been a printer. Within a month the Gilbertese people had their Gospel of Matthew.

In the midst of the thousand and one daily tasks of the missionary Bingham never lost sight of his goal of the Bible for the Gilbert Islands, and at last after forty years he completed it, giving to yet another tribe the whole counsel of God.

Translation work did not end with the close of "the Missionary Century." The deepening sense of the need for the Word of God and the strategic importance of the printed page have made the translator's task continually more significant. The number of those who continue "to bear Glad Tidings" is still on the increase.

CHAPTER 8

THEY BEAR
GLAD TIDINGS

There are hundreds of men and women who today are carrying on the noble tradition of early missionary pioneers. It would be helpful if we could describe a typical present-day translator, but there is no such person. Translators are as different as night and day. A few are "men of the desk" who dedicate themselves almost exclusively to translation and scholarly productions; but most of them are busy evangelists who snatch precious minutes from their work among the people to translate some Bible portion for the coming Sunday, or medical missionaries who, after long hours of ministering to the overwhelming physical needs of the people, translate by the flickering lamp into the wee hours of the night, because they realize that the spiritual requirements of the people surpass by far their physical needs. Some Bible translators are outstanding scholars—students of theology, linguistics, and anthropology—who bring to their work the rich exegetical treasures of Biblical scholarship. There are others who have only a minimum of training, but their personal devotion to the claims of Christ has led them to consecrate their lives to translating the Word of Life into some unknown tongue. We need to have a glance at some of the men and women who are struggling with the very problems which this book describes and who have themselves contributed many of the most striking illustrations cited in the following chapters.

Efrain S. Alphonse was piloting the Methodist missionary's small boat through dangerous reefs and up treacherous streams along the northeast coast of Panama. "How would you like to teach school in one of these Valiente Indian villages?" the missionary asked. Efrain thought about the well-known reputation of these fierce people which had gained them the name "Valiente," meaning "brave" and "warlike." What was more, he did not know a word of their language, nor did they know any Spanish. But his friendship for the missionary and his loyalty to Jesus Christ made him realize that something should be done for these neglected peoples so near Efrain's own home in Bocas del Toro.

Accordingly, Efrain, a Negro lad whose father had come to Panama for work on the canal, accepted his post at the age of nineteen and went to live in one of the Indian villages. He knew that he would not be able to teach Valiente people unless they first taught him. So the first day of school began with his trying to learn the Valiente names for such objects as chair, bench, tree, house, boy, girl, canoe, and paddle. Later came the task of figuring out the complicated verbs. How was he to distinguish between the present, the past, and the future forms? This was done by dropping chalk on the ground and carefully noting the comments of the children. The language was not analyzed in a day, nor learned fully in a year. But before long Efrain was offering five cents to anyone who would give him any word which he did not know. In order to master the vocabulary thoroughly, he put together all the possible combinations of consonants and vowels which could form roots and then asked the old men which of these had meaning and what the meaning was. The twelve years which Alphonse spent among the Valientes, living as they lived and coming to understand the rich lore of legend and tribal history, prepared him in a remarkable way for the task of reducing the language to writing and translating two of the Gospels into the language.

Some time was taken out for further training, including seminary, where Alphonse became a thorough student of the Greek New

Testament. At last, he was ready to translate seriously, and with eagerness he revised and corrected his early amateur work and completed portions not previously undertaken. When finally the manuscript was complete, one of his superiors tossed it aside and suggested that he get on with more important work. Nevertheless, the books were published by the Bible Society.

Later a need arose in Jamaica, and Alphonse responded by becoming the pastor of one of the large congregations of the island, with the understanding that someone else should be found to carry on the Valiente work. But year after year passed, and there was no one who would go to the Valientes and stay to minister to the needs of the growing church. At last, Alphonse returned with his family to Panama. Today he continues to shepherd his Valiente flock, who with only two Gospels to guide them during these years in which they were cut off from human help, nevertheless almost doubled in numbers.

Despite a serious heart ailment, which would hospitalize some men, Alphonse carries on his translation of the rest of the New Testament, visits the Valiente villages, directs the five schools and churches, and tries to meet the constant demands which come for his ministry to various English and Spanish-speaking congregations in the Caribbean. Of all the missionary translators in the Western Hemisphere probably no one has entered more fully into the rich realms of aboriginal speech than this humble Negro servant of God who continues his untiring work among a needy people.

A stocky man in tropical shorts stands chatting with a group of naked Dinka workmen along the wharf at Malakal, nestled on the bank of the Nile in the midst of interminable swamps stretching from the mountains of Ethiopia to the Nuba Hills. Wherever this short, unassuming Australian goes, he finds friends among the tall, haughty Dinkas, for he has ministered to their needs for more than thirty years, as a doctor to heal their bodies and as an evangelist to bring them the healing message for their souls.

When Dr. R. Trudinger began his work no one had analyzed the complicated tones and numerous vowels of the language (see page 30. The subtle changes in deceptively similar vowels and the minute, but meaningful, variations in the tones constituted an almost insuperable barrier to reaching the people. Furthermore, the Dinkas did not appreciate having strangers among them. They have always considered their way of life infinitely superior to any importation from the outside, and have combined the pride of the ancient Pharaohs (whose monolithic statues some of them strikingly resemble) with an elaborate religious and social structure, which has made them almost impenetrable for the gospel.

Dr. Trudinger spent year after year among them, and still there were no converts—no one who would put Jesus in the place of ancient gods or haunting spirits. For weeks and months at a time Dr. Trudinger lived in their grass-thatched mud huts, sleeping around the smoldering dung fires in the cattle barns with the men who guarded their cattle. Patiently he ministered to their physical needs and mastered their language as he listened each night to the endless tales of ancient exploits, fights with lions, and magic incantations to overcome malignant spirits. At last he gained a command of the language and learned to understand the mind and thought of the people. He told them more and more of Jesus, who came to earth as the Son of God to reconcile men to God. Few people paid any attention, but finally one and then another accepted. But months and even years would go by without anyone else turning to the Saviour of men. Nevertheless, despite the fierce heat of the sun-baked plains, scorched under the tropical sun during the dry season, and the humid sultriness of the endless swamps during the torrential rains of summer, and despite the fearful annoyance of swarms of mosquitoes, Dr. Trudinger stayed on.

Dr. "True" (as he is called by all of his friends) was never content to do a superficial job. His medical training had taught him thoroughness, and so in approaching the language he went about it in the same way. He formed a dictionary with numerous fine shades of

THEY BEAR GLAD TIDINGS

meaning carefully distinguished; he wrote the tones on the words with accuracy; he organized a grammar so that others might find their way in the maze of unusual word orders and unfamiliar uses of verbs and adjectives; and finally he translated the entire New Testament into the Ngok dialect of Dinka. Dr. Trudinger knew that if medicine was to do any good it had to be assimilated, and so with his translation. In the most difficult portions of the Pauline Epistles he sought to make the grammar so plain and the word usage so natural that Dinkas could clearly understand Paul's message as though it had been written just for them. Rather than teach the people only the Gospels, as some missionaries are content to do, Dr. Trudinger has spent days and weeks instructing congregations of Dinkas in the spiritual life as portrayed in such books as Ephesians and Colossians; for if Paul found that the message as contained in his Epistles was important for the churches of Asia Minor which had just recently been freed from the bonds of idolatry and mystery religions, how much more did the Dinkas need this same teaching!

At a recent gathering of some of the believers along the Sobat, one young leader, who had learned to read the Scriptures almost entirely by teaching himself, ended his testimony with the simple words, "I will never give up my faith in God and the Lord Jesus. If people were to say to me, 'Give up your faith or we will kill you,' I would have to say, 'Kill me, if you will, for He is more than life to me.'"

These words reflect the way in which the beloved Dr. Trudinger has revealed by selfless kindness and consecrated teaching the matchless Saviour of men.

Translators are usually individualists, but Gregorio Choque and Justino Chispe are able to work together to form one of the best partnerships in Bible translating work.

Some years ago the Gospels and Acts had been published in Aymara, the language of about one million Indians in the highlands of Peru and Bolivia. But this early work was in great need of revision, and the rapidly growing congregations needed the rest of the New Testament. A committee was formed of busy nationals and missionaries, most of them from the capital city of La Paz. They were well acquainted with the Aymara spoken in a more or less "corrupted form" in the native quarters of the sprawling capital. But they apparently did not give adequate consideration to the speech of the countless villages dotting the treeless, windswept plains. Consequently they paid relatively little attention to the protests of such people as Gregorio and Justino, who objected to the inadequate and inaccurate renderings.

When proof sheets came back to the Bible Society from Gregorio and his colleague (the rest of the committee were too busy to look into such matters), there were more than six hundred changes in spelling, word order, and the use of words. Obviously something was wrong. Gregorio and Justino were themselves discouraged and downhearted, for they did not want to make so many changes, and yet these were necessary in order to correct only the more glaring mistakes. The earlier translation was an almost word-for-word rendering of the Spanish, and they knew very well that any good sentence in Aymara would reserve the verb for the end. The awkward literalism was the reason why people like old Cisco in the Guatajata congregation used to go off to sleep during the reading of the Scripture, for he admitted quite frankly, "Well, I can't understand it anyway."

But finally there was a chance to change everything. Gregorio and Justino were told that they were to be responsible for making every word, phrase, and sentence sound just as though an Aymara had been speaking or writing. The thoughts were to be the thoughts as expressed in the Spanish, which these men knew, but the language was to be in every way their own mother tongue.

Gregorio and Justino were schoolteachers and lay leaders in the congregation of Guatajata, on the shores of Lake Titicaca, the highest navigable lake in the world. Many years before a wealthy Italian traveler had been so touched by the depressing misery of the economically enslaved Indians on the huge highland estates that he had left money in Bolivia for some responsible group to buy a farm, liberate the Indians, and give them a chance to live as free men. At last the Canadian Baptist Mission assumed this responsibility and bought the eroded, run-down hacienda of Guatajata. Soon schools were erected, a medical dispensary was functioning, a farm was teaching improved agricultural methods, people were released from the generations of enslaving debt, and the Good News was being preached in the villages huddled along the reed-banked shores of the lake.

Gregorio Choque and Justino Chispe graduated from the schools opened by the missionaries and then took up the task of teaching school in near-by villages. Their keen minds, open hearts, and judicious leadership made them outstanding both in the school and in the church. They were released from their duties to dedicate themselves completely to the revision of the New Testament. Day after day they sat across the desk from each other. Gregorio would read the manuscript while Justino checked the Spanish. Then they discussed each phrase. Was that the right order of the words? Did the pronouns indicate just who was speaking and who was spoken to? If not, nouns would be used in place of pronouns to make the meaning clear. Would the people over on the other side of the lake in Peru understand the words, or would only the Bolivian Aymaras use such a form? These were the kinds of questions asked and answered. Many times they consulted the local pastor, Modesto Ariaga, or went to the missionaries for help on technical details and subtle distinctions in meaning.

After months of thorough, painstaking work, they submitted a manuscript which not only spoke the language of the people but as regards details of punctuation and spelling was one of the best ever received by the American Bible Society. With the manuscript came a letter expressing thanks to God for the privilege of working on the revision of the New Testament in their language. This had been a service of love and a debt of gratitude, for as Justino put it so simply,

"Since the Good News has come to us, it is as though Jesus Christ were living in our villages."

To the east of Java lies the tourist-famous, exotic Isle of Bali, primitive in its luxuriant beauty and ancient in its fierce conservatism, which repulsed the influence of Islam and clung tenaciously to the ancient religion of India, enriched by native symbolism and intriguing dance motifs. The fanatical opposition of local rulers had closed the doors of Bali to all missionary work, until a Chinese missionary under the direction of the Christian and Missionary Alliance entered there in 1932 in order to work among the thousands of Chinese residents in the islands. Some of the Balinese wives, however, also believed the Good News, and this missionary had to be withdrawn, but not before about eight hundred people had accepted the message of Him who died that men might live.

In order that the people of Bali and especially the Christian converts might have the Word of God, the Netherlands Bible Society sent out one of their outstanding Bible translators, Dr. J. L. Swellengrebel, who had prepared for this work for a number of years. The training of this tall blond Dutchman in his twenties included not only the usual academic work in Holland, during which time he studied Latin, Greek, English, French, and German, but he had taken up Classical Arabic, Sanskrit, Javanese, Malay, Comparative Indonesian, and had done some linguistic work on Batta, spoken in Sumatra, and on Bare'e, spoken in the Central Celebes. He also had a thorough preparation in cultural anthropology, and the study of ancient Javanese and Balinese cultures gave him the indispensable tools with which to undertake his important task of giving to the Balinese people the Word of God in their own language.

The Balinese are no crude primitive people with only a few meager cultural accomplishments. Their patterns of life are richly embedded in an old tradition, which is expressed by an immense vocabulary and very subtly reflects the social stratification of an old society by the many special terms and forms which characterize all the important social ranks. Giving the Bible to the Balinese would be no task for a novice. All of Dr. Swellengrebel's study in Old Balinese and Old Javanese, which was the field of his doctoral dissertation accepted by the University of Leiden, proved not only important but highly practical for the complex task to which God had called him.

It was not only necessary for Dr. Swellengrebel to learn to speak Balinese well, but it was equally obligatory to study the rich literary tradition, to form an adequate dictionary, and to study the ethnological setting of the words and phrases, especially those which had to do with the elaborate religious life of a society in which religious practice and social custom had been so intrinsically interwoven. The first five years were spent largely in this fundamental, essential work. But then came the Japanese invaders, who destroyed all the language notes—the labor of five years. They took Dr. Swellengrebel off to a prisoner-of-war camp in Singapore and thrust his family in a concentration camp in Java. For five long years Dr. Swellengrebel lived at the mercy of the Japanese camp commanders.

After a reunion with his family and a brief visit to his home in the Netherlands, he returned to Bali to begin again. Of course, the work went more rapidly the second time, and in about three years, more than fifteen files of card-index data had been reassembled and the Gospel of Luke was completed. But again he was forced to leave Bali. This time it was because of local political tension, which made it better for the native church not to have a foreigner near by. But in Java he continued his work on the New Testament.

Candelaria Camargo is not what one would call a Bible translator, but she is typical of the scores of native Christian workers who wish to put the Scriptures into written form in their own mother tongue. Candelaria is a Quechua Indian from the valley of Junín, where the liberation forces fought one of the most decisive battles for the freedom of the New World from the domination of Spain. Most of the people in this valley, however, still remain enslaved by ignorance.

As a child she heard about Jesus Christ from a colporteur who visited her bleak village and told of the love of God for all people, including little children. Her cruel, fanatical father opposed her at every turn, but at last, despite persecution and threats, she was baptized and became one of the leaders in the local congregation.

Candelaria's face is heavy, ridged, and square. Her coarse black hair drawn back tightly from her face accentuates the deep-cut features, as prominent as the jagged peaks that surround the Junín plateau and as firm as the frozen tundra in the icy mountain passes. And yet, the joy of her smile and the warmth of her kind eyes reveal a compassionate heart and selfless soul.

The pastor in her village church remained only a short time, leaving after the death of his wife and the ill health of his child. Candelaria alone remained to take up the task of ministering to the spiritual needs of scattered congregations in the haciendas, mining camps, and mountain valleys high above the timber line. At one time she was the only preacher for twenty-seven churches, ten of which she organized herself. To reach these congregations she had to travel almost entirely by foot, trudging over mountain passes 15,000 and 16,000 feet high, braving driving snows and freezing rains to bring the message of what Christ could do in her life and theirs.

Her only training had been the yearly Bible conferences and the infrequent opportunities to hear missionaries and other workers who passed through her region. But her heart was never satisfied with the message in Spanish. So many of the Quechuas in Junín could not understand the Spanish, and their dialect of Quechua was so different from the others that translations in the other dialects were not usable. Candelaria's preaching and teaching consisted primarily in taking the Scriptures as she read them in Spanish and then attempting to interpret these in Quechua to her own people. But she realized fully how inadequate this was. Consequently she was overjoyed when finally someone could teach her how to write her own language, using the Spanish alphabet in so far as it was adaptable, but adding certain symbols and combinations to fill out the extra sounds of her own language. With the help of her brothers, who had a better knowledge of Spanish, she tried to render the Good News into the language of Junín. Her unskilled efforts needed guidance, but she struggled on, despite sickness and disappointments, so that eventually the congregations in the cloud-swept plains of Junín could have the Word of God in their own mother tongue.

The task of the true translator is one of identification. As a Christian servant he must identify himself with Christ; as a translator he must identify himself with the Word; as a missionary he must identify himself with the people. The Rev. J. A. Persson from Sweden, working among the Tswa people of South Africa and Mozambique, so identified himself with those whom he went to serve that at a farewell dinner given in his honor before a furlough one Tswa man arose and paid the highest tribute a white man could ever receive in Africa: "Mr. Persson may have a white skin, but his heart is as black as any of us." The translator must be a man *of* the people if he wishes to translate *for* the people.

CHAPTER 9

GOD SPEAKS TO
THE HEART

If the message of the Good News is to reach the heart, it must be presented in the words which speak to the heart. This does not mean the introduction of fanciful metaphors and unknown figures of speech; it means the use of those rich expressions with which the language is already endowed. Missionary translators have discovered hundreds of such expressions, which have become a constant source of spiritual enlightenment and blessing.

Faith and Believe

No two words reach more deeply into the soul and the spirit than do these related terms; in Greek they are simply two different forms of the same basic word. The profoundly personal experience of faith has led in many languages to the employment of words and phrases which attempt to capture and reflect this intimate relationship of the soul to the object of faith and confidence. The Karré people in the forests of the Ubangi-Chari district of French Equatorial Africa speak of "faith" as "to hear and take into the soul." Simple "hearing" is not enough. Men may hear with deaf ears and rejecting hearts. The Karrés have perceived that the essence of faith consists in this acceptance, not merely in outward appearance, but in taking the truth "into the soul." Their neighbors, the Kabba-Lakas, have emphasized the same truth, but by a slightly different idiom. They say, "to hear within one's self and not let go." Again, it is not the

118

hearing with the ears, but with the heart that counts, and faith leads to "not letting go." In one of the West African languages this double process of taking and keeping is described graphically as "to take the word and eat it." Such assimilation of the truth, so that it becomes a part of ourselves, is the very message of the Scriptures.

The Lacandon Indians, a tribe of a few hundred people scattered in the dense jungles of southern Mexico and Guatemala at the base of the Yucatan Peninsula, say that "to believe God" is "to cause God's word to enter one's heart." Note that there is here no side-stepping of the human responsibility in the process of faith. We say that men must "open their hearts" to God, for God will not force Himself upon men. The Lacandons recognize this fact unconsciously by the very causative form of the verb, which indicates clearly man's part in the triumph of faith. The Uduks along the Ethiopian border express essentially the same truth as the Lacandons, but in slightly different words, when they say that "to believe God" is "to join God's word to the body." This is the faith of living reality—not just accepting God's word, but "joining it to the body," making this union of belief and action, which alone constitutes real faith.

The Conob Indians, living in the high mountains along the northern frontier of Guatemala, speak of "faith" as "truth entering into one's soul."[1] This expression points to the same essential truth, namely, that faith touches the heart and soul. It is not the formulation of the mind or the outward assent to ritualistic dogma; it is the experience of the innermost being.

Some of the languages of West Africa tell the same story about "faith," but in somewhat different forms. The Mossi people around Ouagadougou in French West Africa speak of "faith" as "leaning on God." This would seem to be faith, confidence, trust, and dependence all included in one phrase. But this is a truth which more sophisticated believers have ignored. It has been the unfortunate fact of history that men have warped this truth about "leaning on

---

[1] Literally this word may be translated "abdomen," but it is functionally equivalent to English "soul."

God" and have hypostatized faith as a series of man-made dogmas, and then, as in the time of the Inquisition, they have even fought and killed their fellow men because these refused to bow before such word-idols. It has been so easy to wrest the word "faith" from its meaning of constant and continual dependence upon God and Jesus Christ to one in which "faith" becomes "the faith," the embodiment of statements about truth, and not Him who was and is "the Way, the Truth, and the Life." The declaration of our faith is most important, but it must never be permitted to obscure our dependence upon the Risen Christ. In a near-by language the act of faith is described as "committing oneself to be held." This is the same phrase which is used to describe the act of a mother who tenderly commits her child into the arms of someone else while she must be occupied with other tasks. This likewise is the experience of dependence, based upon confidence and trust.

In the Aztec dialect spoken in the region of Zacapoaxtla, Mexico, "faith" is described as "following close after." This figure of speech is derived from the trail. Faith in a person means that we follow close behind him. We have confidence that he can lead us correctly; and that as we follow in his footsteps, we shall be safe. Faith is not a substance which can be purchased or hoarded. Faith is an act, and "following close after" describes our proper relationship to Him in a most vivid way.

The Valiente Indians of Panama describe "faith" in a rather strange way. They say that it is "catching God in the mind." Some might prefer a phrase which would indicate God's act of catching us, but this Valiente figure of speech does convey an important truth. It is derived from the experience of hunting animals in the forest. This involves a careful procedure of spying out, tracking down, and finally catching—that is, making it one's own possession. In a sense this can also be the experience of faith. After careful observation and watching, we finally make that spiritual grasp for the reality of faith—and it becomes ours. One must not imagine that the Valientes think of hunting God down, but "in the mind" they can "catch God."

The Shipibo Indians in Peru say that "to believe on God" is "to be strong on God." This phrase does not mean precisely what it might appear to mean from the literal rendering in English. It actually means that there is no strength at all without Him. That is to say, we are strong only in reliance upon God. One cannot be spiritually strong except by dependence upon God. For the Shipibos, spiritual strength is a completely derived strength. There is no place for spiritual pride about one's personal power. This is ruled out by the language itself, for strength is "on God."

The Piro Indians, who live to the south of their Shipibo neighbors, say that to believe is literally "to obey-believe." For them the verb "believe" is too weak to express belief in God, since such a "faith" could be about the mere truth of occurrence—just admitting that something did or did not happen. This type of intellectual belief has always been found insufficient to describe the faith in Jesus Christ, which includes not only the intellectual assent to certain facts about the Lord but the opening of the heart to communion and fellowship with one whose Lordship demands complete obedience. Accordingly, the Piros, by means of a compound word, have tried to express this union of "faith" and "works"— believing and obeying, without which there is no reality to Christian experience and no message in the Good News.

The Timorese people of Indonesia have emphasized another aspect of "faith." They describe it in the words "to conform with the heart." The essential meaning of this phrase would push the reality of "faith" just a step further than some expressions. It not only implies acceptance of truth, but conformance to truth by the one whose heart responds to its claims. This is in very essence the Christian concept of faith, for without conformance there is no faith. Furthermore, this conformance must not be purely a matter of external practices, but of the heart. The heart determines action, and not action the heart.

The Huichol Indians on the western slopes of central Mexico describe faith in somewhat similar terms, but their expression emphasizes the objective more than the subjective aspects of conformity. They say that "to believe" is "to conform to the truth." This is not very different from the Timorese idiom. In fact, the truth of faith might be defined as a blend of both these ideas: "conforming to the truth with the heart."

The Loma people in the hinterland of Liberia, West Africa, use still another means of describing "faith." As a translation of "to have faith in the gospel" they say literally, "to lay one's hand on the Good News." This phrase reflects the Loma practice of identifying oneself with an object or action by "laying one's hand on it," that is, indicating to all who witness the act that here is one who completely identifies himself with the truth for which he stands. True faith is then not something which can be hidden. In its very nature it must be clearly evident as one identifies himself with the object of his faith. This is the truth of Romans 10:10, "confession is made unto salvation."

Trust

"Trust" is so closely related to "faith" that it can scarcely be isolated from it. The Mayan Indians of Yucatan express the active process of "entrusting oneself to God" as "putting oneself upon God." Trusting is not a mere aimless hope, conceived in an atmosphere of mild desperation. It is the process of committing oneself to something or someone more real and sure. To trust God means "to put oneself upon God."

But not only may men trust, they may refuse to trust God. To describe this state the San Blas Indians of Panama are bluntly frank. They say that a man has "doubts within him." We sometimes gloss over any lack of trust and confidence in God by describing it as a kind of vacuum experience of the soul. This idea is impossible in San Blas. Lack of trust does not consist in the absence of trust, but in the presence of doubt. Spiritual life is not made up of zeros (significant absences of something), but of positive elements—either for or against. Those who do not live by faith live in doubt; and doubts are real.

Doubt

For so many people "doubt" implies a hazy uncertainness, a kind of meaningless worry, or an anxious state of the mind, where thoughts never seem to find their proper places. In some languages "doubt" is more positively described. The Huanuco Quechuas, on the eastern slopes of the lofty Peruvian Andes, describe "doubt" very accurately by the simple phrase "to have two thoughts." The Shipibos, living farther to the east, have practically the same expression, "to think two things." There is a sense in which doubt may distribute itself among scores of alternatives, but fundamentally doubt consists of that eternal equation expressed in such simple words by Shakespeare: "To be or not to be." Doubt implies "it is or it is not," being "for or against," choosing "this or that."

The Kekchi language, spoken in the state of Alta Verapaz in Guatemala, describes this conflict between opposing concepts by the phrase "his heart is made two." Doubt splits the personality and keeps one from following positive programs. It accounts for the spiritual duality and conflict which exist in so many immature Christians. The Navajo Indians in the southwestern United States describe doubt in practically the same terms by saying "that which is two is with him."

Doubt may be described, however, in other ways. It is not always the simple alternative which is presented to the spiritual pilgrim. As one journeys along the road of life there are many points at which numerous paths lead off, and apparently into equally attractive areas. As a result we are confused and begin to doubt the reality of our former experience and guidance. Or we may discover that there is no road ahead. We have apparently chosen a blind alley. And our faith disappears. To describe this kind of doubt the Baouli people of the Ivory Coast in West Africa have an excellent phrase "my thoughts are not upon it." If one's thoughts are upon some-thing, there is confidence; if not, there is doubt.

The Piros of Peru have still another way of describing "doubt." They say it is "to have a hard heart." The impenetrable heart cannot be convinced. Its stubborn defiance can only lead to doubt. Faith implies receptivity; doubt is the fortress of the self-sufficient, defiant soul.

Worry

Doubt leads to worry as surely as evening shadows lead to night. As we noted on page 24, the Navajo Indians rightly describe worry as "my mind is killing me." The Piros in Peru use almost the same idiom when they say that a worried man is "one who is hard chased." The worried person is like a pursued animal in the forest trying to elude the hunter. The impenetrable jungle of the future, the failing strength, and the exhaustion of doubt all press hard upon the soul. And one's heart seems to fail and even disappear. This is the very phrase employed by the Tzeltal Indians in the rugged mountains of southern Mexico. They describe "worry" by the words "their hearts are gone." In so many instances worry is the spiritual sin of the self-occupied soul, but one cannot engage in such self-centered concern without being robbed of something precious— even one's own heart. The center of worry is always self, and "he who would try to keep his own soul, shall lose it" (Matthew 16:25).

Confidence

Confidence is the antidote for worry, but confidence is not born of wishful thinking. It comes from knowing. The Navajos describe confidence by the very process through which it is obtained, namely, "tracking down to the end." If a horse has wandered off down a bush-lined arroyo, the only way to know about this horse is carefully to follow its hoofprints, tracking it down until it has been found. Confidence in the truth of the gospel does not arise from idle speculation about possible truths. It consists in "tracking down to the end" that which we wish to make the object of our confidence. Confidence implies not blind submission but active investigation. Confidence is born of experience.

Love

There is no gospel without love, even as there is no life without faith. But the life of faith not only results from the reconciliation of Calvary which proceeded from love, but it is also sustained by love. This is not only God's love for us, but our love for Him, which is the basis of all communion and our highest spiritual joy. The terms for "love," even more than for "faith," reflect the inner subjective consciousness.

The Habbé people on the edge of the Sahara in French West Africa speak of "love for God" as "to put God in our hearts." This does not mean that God can be contained wholly within the heart of a man, but the Eternal does live within the hearts of men by His Holy Spirit, and it is only love which prompts the soul to "put God in the heart."

The Zapotec Indians of the Mitla dialect, nestled in the mountains of Oaxaca, Mexico, describe "love" in almost opposite words. Instead of putting God into one's own heart, they say, "my heart goes away with God." Both the Habbés and the Zapotecs are right. There is a sense in which God dwells within us, and there is also a sense in which out hearts are no longer our own. They belong to Him, and the object of affection is not here on earth, but as pilgrims with no certain abiding place we long for that fuller fellowship of heaven itself.

The Uduks seem to take a rather superficial view of love, for they speak of it as "good to the eye." But we must not judge spiritual insight or capacity purely on the basis of idioms. Furthermore, there is a sense in which this idiom is quite correct. In fact the Greek term *agapê*, which is used primarily with the meaning of love of God and of the Christian community, means essentially "to appreciate the worth and value of something." It is not primarily the love which arises from association and comradeship (this is *philê*),[2] but it defines that aspect of love which prompted God to love us when there was no essential worth or value in us, except as we could be remade in the image of His Son. Furthermore, it is the love which must prompt us to see in men and women, still unclaimed for Jesus Christ, that which God can do by the working of His Spirit. This is the love which rises higher than personal interests and goes deeper than sentimental attachment. This is the basis of the communion of the saints.

Love may sometimes be described in strong, powerful terms. The Miskitos of the swampy coasts of eastern Nicaragua and Honduras say that "love" is "pain of the heart." There are joys which become so intense that they seem to hurt, and there is love which so dominates the soul that its closest emotion seems to be pain. The Tzotzils, living in the cloud-swept mountains of Chiapas in southern Mexico, describe love in almost the same way as the Miskitos. They say it is "to hurt in the heart." Accordingly, John 3:16 reads, "God so hurt in his heart, that he gave his only Son. . . ." The love of God for sinful man must surely have caused the heart of God to hurt, and yet it was not the pain of hurt feelings but the compassion of an open heart which sought in Christ to reconcile the world unto Himself.

The Conob Indians of northern Guatemala have gone even a step further. They describe love as "my soul dies." Love is such that, without experiencing the joy of union with the object of our love, there is a real sense in which "the soul dies." A man who loves God according to the Conob idiom would say "my soul dies for God." This not only describes the powerful emotion felt by the one who loves, but it should imply a related truth—namely, that in true love there is no room for self. The man who loves God must die to self. True love is of all emotions the most unselfish, for it does not look out for self but for others. False love seeks to possess; true love

---

[2] See page 63 for a fuller discussion of these Greek words translated "love."

seeks to be possessed. False love leads to cancerous jealousy; true love leads to a life-giving ministry.

Well Pleased

In Mark 1:11 "love" and "well pleased" become two aspects of one great single declaration: "Thou are my beloved Son, in whom I am well pleased." Good pleasure follows after love as the morning sunshine fulfills the hope of a glorious sunrise. The Neao people of Liberia translate this "well pleased" as "my heart rests in you." The near-by Loma people say "my heart lies down with you." Here is confident joy which prompts a desire for fellowship.

The Pame Indians, living in the bleak, eroded mountains of central Mexico, describe this emotion somewhat differently. They say "you pull at my heart." This pulling is not the tug of pity—as we might assume from the English equivalent—it is the pull toward communion and the joy of association.

The Piros employ another phrase. They say "my thoughts are arranged." No longer is one possessed by discordant, unharmonious distractions and contradictions or troubled by doubts and worries. The thoughts have been arranged, that is, put in their proper places, and hence one is "well pleased." This is an aspect of the spiritual life which we too often neglect. In the clutter of distractions there is no basis of spiritual fellowship.

Anger

We generally think of "anger" in terms of what it does to others, not what it does to ourselves. It may then come as a shock to us to realize that in some languages it is this subjective aspect of anger which comes to the fore. The Mende people of West Africa speak of anger as "a cut heart," and the Miskito Indians say that it is "a split heart." This "split heart" is not merely the result of the offense which we have suffered; it results from the antagonism which we permit to dominate our emotions.

The Tzotzils in Chiapas, Mexico, say that "anger" consists in "having a hot heart." This is a rather accurate description of the emotion which we feel. The Conobs just across the border in Guatemala say that it is "a red soul" (or literally, "insides"). The flushed face of the angry man must indicate a red interior from which the anger comes. The Mossi people of West Africa say simply that an angry man has "a swollen heart."

Peace

There is a negative and a positive peace. The negative peace is an absence of war. The positive peace consists of a quiet confidence in God as ruler and sustainer of the universe. A translation of the negative meaning is simple enough—"no war." The translation of the positive element of peace involves a wide selection of word pictures, each depicting some special aspect of peace.

One of the most common types of metaphors is the one used by the Gbeapo people of Liberia. They say "my heart sits down." There is no longer any need of anxious wandering to and fro in the midst of life's uncertainties. One's heart may sit down in the confidence that God controls the past, the present, and the future. The Lacandons, living in small family groups in tropical jungles of southern Mexico, say that peace is "rest within." It is not the rest of body but the rest of soul. The Zapotec Indians in the mountains near Oaxaca City in Mexico add a further aspect. They say that peace is "the heart sitting quiet." Repose of the heart is regarded as insufficient. Quietness must be the essence of its repose.

In the Cuicatec language of Mexico "peace" is translated by the word "quietness," but from the context it is quite obvious that the Scriptures are speaking of that quietness which characterizes the spirit, not just the environment. One might regard the translation of "quietness" as insufficient—certainly there are other more expressive metaphors—and yet if Christians could only learn the simple truth of this translation, they would be profited immeasurably. Many people strive desperately hard to find "peace of mind" or "peace of soul." But they never stop in the anxious hubbub of their lives to be quiet long enough for God to speak to them. He does not speak through the excitement of artificial living in our so-called civilized world. He continues to speak in the still small voice, which we drown out by the pathetic noisiness of our fruitless lives.

The Valiente Indians describe peace as "having a quiet mind." Noisy minds are restless minds, and restless minds are usually in rebellion—either against the world or against God. In the Kekchi language of Guatemala one perceives the entrance of a positive element into the description of peace in the phrase "quiet goodness." Peace is not passive, but active—that is, active in quietness.

In a number of places in Africa "peace" is described as a kind of coolness. The Futa-Fula people in French Guinea describe "peace" simply as "coolness." It is no wonder that "peace" should be described as "coolness" by those who know the hot blasts of wind coming from the Sahara and the humid storms from the coasts. Peace comes with new hope to the anxious, worried soul even as the cool evening breeze brings new life to scorched trees and grass.

Certain aspects of peace are not covered by word pictures based upon "rest" or upon "coolness." The Zacapoaxtla Aztecs in Mexico describe peace as being "completeness." One who is not at peace with God, others, or himself is not complete. He is lacking in something, they say. And they are right. Anxiety and worry are evidences of deformed, incomplete souls, which experience only a partial existence. The Miskitos of Nicaragua and Honduras describe substantially the same characteristic by the phrase "to have one heart." The peaceful man has just one heart. He is not divided in his loyalties, nor incomplete in his personality. Note that peace contrasts with doubt. The doubting man is one who has two hearts —or maybe more; but the peaceful man has only one, and with that he is complete.

The Piros, who use the phrase "my thoughts are arranged" to describe "good pleasure" (see page 127), speak of peace as a quality of "the well-arranged soul." That which is "well arranged" is regarded by the Piros as beautiful. Thus the peaceful man is one who may be said to have a beautiful soul. It is no wonder that so many people live anxious lives when their souls contain such an ugly clutter of discordant emotions: selfish ambition and noble altruism, sensuous pleasures and holy aspirations, haunting memory and hopeful expectancy.

Peace is also akin to joy, and this is recognized by the Baouli people of the Ivory Coast when they say that peace is "a song in the body," while joy is "a song in the stomach." The "song in the body" is a more all-pervading experience; joy is something more temporary.

Patience

Peace is the quality of the soul; patience is the behavior of the soul. The Aymara Indians of Bolivia have described patience well by the phrase "a waiting heart."

The Valientes of Panama describe patience in more vivid terms. They say that it is "chasing down your temper." The impatient person lets his temper run away with him. Patience requires one to "chase down his temper" and get it under control.

The Mayas describe patience as "strength not to fall." This seems to include almost more than patience, but it is important to note that this Mayan translation recognizes that impatience means "falling." For some of us, who tend to take a certain secret pride in our impatience—describing it as energetic drive—it might be well to recognize that impatience is failure, while patience is strength.

The San Blas Indians in Panama use a rather strange phrase to depict patience. They say "not caring what happens." But this is not meant as condoning foolhardy indifference to life and danger. It reflects a kind of reckless confidence in God, a confidence not bred of desperation but of utter reliance. The patient person is not concerned about what happens; he is willing to wait in confidence.

Sorrow

Sorrow touches the very center of the human personality. The Mossi people in West Africa say that sorrow means "a spoiled heart."

The neighboring Bambaras describe sorrow as "a blackening of the eyes." Conversely happiness "whitens the eyes." This is not a reference to the use of paint to show sorrow or gladness, but the colors black and white characterize the emotional states of sorrow and joy.

Intense sorrow and trouble is expressed in the Kabba-Laka language of French Equatorial Africa as "my soul is seeking me." By this phrase the Kabba-Laka people indicate their belief in the possibility of the soul wandering off in its grief and distraction, and then seeking its possessor again. This is not an uncommon way of describing intense, emotional suffering, which seems to split the personality and drive its various parts in different directions. The anguish suffered during the time in which the person is finding himself again is intensified by a desperate anxiety, since failure to be reunited is regarded as resulting in insanity or death.

Despair

A person in despair is described by the Conob Indians as "one who has fallen in his soul."

The apparent inescapable catastrophe for the soul is depicted in the Gilbertese language, spoken in the Gilbert Islands of Micronesia, by a phrase quite similar to ours, "my mind is at an end."

Consolation

For those in despair there is still consolation. One reads in the Tarascan language, spoken in Mexico, "God takes sadness from our hearts," that is, "He consoles us." This is such a simple way of speaking about consolation, but there is a finality about this phrase which gives it power. If we could only read with faith Philippians 2:1 "If therefore Christ takes sadness from the heart . . . ," our faltering step would become a firm stride as we walk with confidence and in the joy of the Spirit.

The Aymara language describes consolation in terms of "preparing the heart." Fundamentally, this is just what we need. Too often we look for compensating blessings, which will recompense us for sorrow and trouble. What we actually need is a "prepared heart."

God does not distribute spiritual candies for spoiled children; He would give us a new and prepared heart.

Compassion

Compassion is the emotional source of consolation. But it is not a form of exaggerated sentimentalism. It is what the word implies in its etymology, namely, "suffering with." This is beautifully suggested in the Shilluk phrase "cries in his soul." The one who has compassion for another "cries in his soul" as he sees the trouble and despair that has befallen his neighbor. And as he does "cry in his soul," he cannot do less than express that compassion in acts of kindness.

Joy

The relationship of joy to "sweetness" is reflected in many idioms. The Bambaras of French West Africa describe joy as "the spirit is made sweet," while the Kpelles, to the south in Liberia, say that joy is "a sweet heart." The Tzeltals in Mexico speak of joy as "the good taste of one's heart." Such widespread distribution of an idiom suggests that there is a close psychological relationship between the pleasure experienced in tasting something sweet and the joy that comes from an abundant life.

Closely related to these expressions for joy are the Uduk phrase "good to the stomach" and Baouli term (noted on page 130) "a song in the stomach." The Miskitos of Nicaragua and Honduras use the rather strange expression, "the liver is wide open"—happily accepting the pleasures flooding in upon it.

Happiness

Distinguishing between "joy" and "happiness" is not easy, but it is interesting to note how in some languages joy is interpreted as more all-pervading and permanent, while happiness is regarded as more temporary and more dependent upon external circumstances. The Valientes of Panama distinguish by the phrases "happy within me" for "joy" and "happy around me" for "happiness." Joy is the happiness which abides within and characterizes the heart, while happiness describes those transitory states which reflect the pleasantness which may surround one.

The concept of "sweetness" is also employed in words for happiness. The Mossi people of West Africa say "my head is sweet," and the Kabba-Lakas of Central Africa declare "my body is sweet." The Lomas of Liberia say "my stomach is sweet," while the near-by Mendes state "my insides are sweet." All of these expressions amount to substantially the same thing: sweetness is happiness, but it is not the sweetness of food, but the sweetness of life.

Hope

Hope is sometimes one of the most difficult terms to translate in the entire Bible. It is not because people do not hope for things, but so often they speak of hoping as simply "waiting." In fact, even in Spanish the word *esperar* means both "to wait" and "to hope." However, in many instances the purely neutral term meaning "to wait" may be modified in such a way that people will understand something more of its significance. For example, in Cuicatec, a language of southern Mexico, hope is called "wait-desire." Hope is thus a blend of two activities: waiting and desiring. This is substantially the type of expectancy of which hope consists.

The Maya language describes the dependence of hope by the phrase "on what it hangs." "Our hope in God" means that "we hang onto God." The object of hope is the support of one's expectant waiting.

Covetousness

The heart is not only capable of noble, pure aspirations, but it seems equally adept at adopting mean and ugly moods. The Tzeltals in Mexico describe a covetous person as "a small-hearted person." Covetousness does involve the shrinking of the personality in proportion as it exalts the values of things and denies the rights of others. The Mayas make no excuses for such a person but say quite bluntly that covetousness is "desiring what others have."

Covetousness is an insatiable appetite which may overwhelm the reason. This is clearly brought out by the Shipibos, who describe a covetous person as "one who has gone crazy for things." This is the kind of psychopathic egoism which induces so many to make idols of material possessions and prostrate their souls before them.

Envy

Envy is bred of covetousness and self-centeredness. The Tzeltals, who recognize a covetous man as having a "small heart" (see page 133), say that an envious person has "a greedy heart." "Small hearts" and "greedy hearts" go together, and the soul shrinks in direct proportion to its greediness. The envious person is never satisfied, for he can never keep step with his own insatiable ego.

The Chontal Indians, living in the low, swampy delta land of Tabasco in southern Mexico, regard envy in a more subtle way. They say of the man who is envious of his neighbor, "He did not want to see his neighbor." This describes the end result of envy. People cannot bear to see others enjoying the privileges which they insist should be their own. The envious man has acquired such a self-directed stare that he cannot take his eyes off self to see another's enjoyment.

Thankfulness

Thankfulness is the great antidote for envy, since it re-establishes the proper relationship among people. In some languages there is no formal way of saying thanks. One must just declare, "It is good!" But there are many languages in which the saying of thanks has taken on quite a formal or even exotic manner of expression. The Mossi people of French West Africa say "my head is in the dirt." This is derived from the custom of expressing thanks by bowing low before another and actually pressing the head into the dirt, so humbled does one feel because of the graciousness of another.

A "thankless person," on the other hand, is a "bill-wiping person." This unusual phrase is derived from observing how chickens after voraciously gobbling down all the food, even to the tiniest kernels and specks, wipe off their bills in two or three hasty movements, and seem to be as hungry as ever. They never stop for a moment to express thanks but become busily engaged in looking for more food. The thankless person is on the lookout for more benefits while he is still "wiping his bill."

The Kabba-Lakas express thankfulness as "grabbing with both hands." This is exactly what the people do when they wish to say, "Thank you!" They grab each other with both hands, and with all the words at their command express their joy and appreciation.

The Mayas take a strictly theological view of thankfulness by saying "May God pay you." In fact, they will use the words *Dios bootik* "God pay you" when speaking to God Himself, and they do not sense any contradiction, for the word has now become a completely petrified formula.

In the Karré language thankfulness to God is expressed as "to sit down on the ground before God." A thankful Karré will go to the home of his benefactor and sit on the ground before his hut. No word need be spoken; it is his silent presence which gives eloquent testimony to his thankfulness. One who is thankful to God is thus encouraged to sit down before God, to enjoy His presence, and to declare one's thankfulness and dependence upon the gracious kindness of the Creator. Those who tend to acknowledge indebtedness to God by simply taking God for granted have much to learn from the attitude indicated in this Karré phrase. God, who is seeking the fellowship of His children, has prepared untold blessings for those willing to take the time "to sit on the ground before Him" to express their thankfulness by seeking communion with Him.

CHAPTER 10

GOD PROVIDES A WAY

Great truths are embodied in great doctrines—the teachings of our Lord, the prophets, and the apostles. These great doctrines must be explained in living, understandable words, for they must bring life by the power of the Spirit of God or they are empty shells and false fronts for hollow lives. The doctrines of repentance, redemption, salvation, grace, justification, and holiness are not theoretical temples built for the admiration and worship of men, but they are the lowly footpaths by which men are led into God's presence along the way which He has provided.

Repentance and Conversion

Repentance can scarcely be discussed without taking into account the experience of conversion, for true repentance is simply the first step in this God-directed process. The Northern Sothos in South Africa describe this relationship as "to become untwisted," which is repentance, and "to retrace one's steps," which is conversion. Sin in the life warps and twists it, gives it a false direction, and perverts its rightful purposes. In the act of repentance a man becomes conscious of all this, and his thoughts become untwisted. But this is not enough. It is possible for him to become overwhelmed by a sense of self-pity, and though he may recognize the tragedy of his failures, he may like Judas go and destroy himself—either by taking his life or by plunging back into a life of even greater degradation. But

136

true repentance, which keeps God and not self in sight, leads to conversion, "retracing one's steps," as the Prodigal returned to the home of his father.

The Balinese language, spoken in Indonesia, describes these related activities of the soul as "putting on a new mind" (repentance) and "putting on a new behavior" (conversion). The verb "to put on" is the same one used for putting on a garment, and it reminds us of the words of Paul in Romans 13:14 "put on the Lord Jesus" and in Ephesians 4:24 "put on the new man." Note, however, that the Balinese makes it quite clear that a "new mind" must precede a "new behavior." There are too many people who imagine that reformed actions will remake distorted minds, but it is the repentant mind which alone can produce converted actions.

The Ngok Dinkas of the Sudan describe the relationship between repentance and conversion in quite simple terms. The first is "to turn the heart" and the second is "to turn the self." Could it be clearer? In the Luvale language of Angola this same truth is described as first "to be sorrowful and turn" and secondly "to return." The San Blas Indians say "to be sorry in the heart" and "to change the heart." These expressions all declare substantially the same truth. Repentance precedes conversion as the conditioning of the soul for the transforming power of God.

The Conobs describe these processes of repentance and conversion first as "to think in the soul" and then "to molt." In the same way as a butterfly breaks from its ugly chrysalis to become a new creature, so the soul changes its entire aspect and can scarcely be recognized. But first one must "think in the soul"—not merely in the head, where men contrive and scheme—but in the soul, where men meet themselves and see themselves. This becomes the conditioning for the transformation of life.

The spiritual pain which accompanies repentance is clearly indicated by the Kekchi Indians of Guatemala, who say that repentance is "pain in the heart." The Baouli people of the Ivory Coast state quite frankly, "It hurts to make you quit it." This is utter honesty and is a prerequisite to any transformation. God does not seek to gloss over sin or polish up our basically sinful natures. He seeks to give us a new heart, in the sense that we must be born again, even as the Master told Nicodemus. But this cannot happen unless men repent—unless, as the Chols of southern Mexico say, "we leave our sin." Repentance must not be regarded purely as spiritual concern for failure; this can lead to remorse. The repentance of the Bible implies desiring a new heart, even as the Greek word *metanoia* means "changed thinking." The Timorese people of Indonesia describe repentance as "turning the heart upside down."

The feeling that repentance involves a kind of turning back to that point from which we started out in sin is reflected in the Pame language of central Mexico which speaks of repentance as "turning back the heart." The Tzeltals are somewhat more explicit. They say "to cause the heart to return because of sin." This returning is not the idle wish for lost opportunities, but a conscious return to God based upon the recognition of sin. To distinguish repentance from conversion the Tzeltals call the latter, "to cause the heart to return to God's presence." The primary anxiety of repentance is sin; the fundamental concern of conversion is God.

Though we have described conversion as following upon repentance, it must not be thought that the conviction of sin is an experience unrelated to the consciousness of God's transforming power. In fact, it is not the consciousness of sin which brings men to Jesus Christ, but it is the recognition of God in Christ which brings men to the full acknowledgment of their sin. Sin is only an unfortunate mistake unless we see it as God sees it, namely, as rebellion against Him.

Redemption

Redemption by the death of Christ is God's way by which the experience of conversion may be effected in the soul through the working of the Spirit of God. Redemption is what has been done for us, even as conversion represents that which is done in us.

Redemption is often described as involving the process of "buying" even as the English word "redeem" suggests. The Kissi people of French Guinea call redemption "buying back." Ownership of some object may be forfeited or lost, but the original owner may redeem his possession by buying it back. So God, who made us for Himself, permitted us to accept or reject Him. In order to reconcile rebellious mankind He demonstrated His redemptive love in the death of His Son on our behalf.

The process of "buying back" is sometimes more explicitly depicted. In the Black Thai language of Indo-China the Redeemer is described as the "Lord-come-seek-buy." This is the Lord who came and sought us, and then bought us for Himself. Just "to buy a person" might imply acquiring a personal slave. But one who comes seeking in order to buy is one who is earnestly looking for the straying sheep who is lost on the mountainside in his own sinful wandering away from the Shepherd of his soul.

The San Blas Indians describe redemption in a more spiritual sense. They say that it consists of "recapturing the spirit." A sinful person is one in rebellion against God, and he must be recaptured by God or he will destroy himself. The need of the spirit is to be captured by God. The tragedy is that too many people find their greatest pleasure in secretly trying to elude God, as though they could find some place in the universe where He could not find them. They regard life as a purely private affair, and they object to the claims of God as presented by the church. They accuse the pastor of interfering with the privacy of their own iniquity. Such souls, if they are to be redeemed, must be "recaptured."

Salvation

Salvation is the subjective reality of the objective fact of redemption. The Shipibos say that it means "to make to live." If the wages of sin is death, then indeed salvation is life—not only life which goes on for eternity, but life which begins now with its eternal qualities. "He that heareth my word, and believeth on him that sent me, hath everlasting life . . . but is passed from death unto life" (John 5:24).

The San Blas Indians are quite explicit about the theological aspects of salvation and say that it means "to receive help for bad deeds." This help is not just any kind of help but help for the soul which has sinned. The Ngok Dinkas of the Sudan describe salvation as help, but they say "help as to his soul" (or literally, "his breath"). Salvation is thus "soul-help."

The Kabba-Lakas take a very personal view of salvation and describe the Saviour as "one who takes us by the hand." This is not only beautiful but spiritually true. Jesus, who throughout His earthly ministry always had time to respond to the individual, personal needs of people, is still the one who may be described as "taking us by the hand" and leading us into the fellowship of the Triune God.

As may be seen, salvation is regarded as much more than an escape. The soul can never be satisfied with an escapist theology. Christ never offers escape from reality, but strength for life; not a way out, but a way up; not patronage, but power.

Reconciliation

Reconciliation describes God's relationship to the great act of redemption and salvation. This was the Good News that Paul proclaimed to the Corinthians, that "God was in Christ, reconciling the world unto himself" (II Corinthians 5:19). Reconciliation implies the rebellion of man and the initiative of God, and in this the Christian message differs from all other religions. Only Christianity takes seriously the problem of sin and recognizes it for what it is—not maladjustment to things, but opposition to God. Only Christianity presents God as taking the initiative in reconciling the world unto Himself.

The Eskimos of Barrow, Alaska, describe reconciliation in the simple terms of "making friends again." That is to say, "God was in Christ making friends again with the world." The Uduks in the Sudan express this same truth, but in the rather interesting phrase "meet, snapping fingers together again." This expression is derived from the Uduks' practice of snapping fingers together when they meet each other. Instead of shaking hands, they extend their thumbs and middle fingers and snap fingers together, but only friends will do this. Men who have something against each other refuse to acknowledge each other in this way. And so it is that the natural man is an enemy of God; he refuses to snap fingers with God, but God has come to reconcile man to Himself and through Jesus Christ has brought man into fellowship with Himself. Man and God may now meet "to snap fingers together again."

The Black Thai of Indo-China employ quite a different figure of speech. They say that reconciliation consists in "rubbing off the corners." This does not refer to social acceptability, but to rubbing off the corners so that two objects, meant for each other, will fit together. Man is regarded as being incapable of fitting into the plan and fellowship of God because of the sin which has deformed him and which stands out as an ugly growth on his personality. The corners of iniquity must be rubbed off so that man may be reconciled to God and made to fit into God's eternal plan for the world.

Forgiveness

Forgiveness constitutes the spiritual medium of reconciliation. The barrier of sin, which has divided man from his Maker, has been broken down by the forgiveness which God manifested in the death of His Son. But it is not easy to find an adequate term to describe this unmerited forgiveness. In the Shipibo language native helpers first suggested the word meaning "to pass over without seeing," but this could imply purely accidental neglect. Another word meaning "not to think of" could mean "avoidance." Still another expression implied the canceling of a debt, but this failed to express fully the spiritual significance of forgiveness. Finally, the term "to rub out" (or "to erase") was selected. This word indicates not only that sin is recognized for what it is, but that God consciously eliminates the guilt of sin so that it exists no more.

The San Blas people go a step further. Forgiveness is spoken of as "erasing the evil heart." It is not only the individual acts of sin which God is thought of as forgiving, but also the guilt of sin which clings to the heart. "To erase the evil heart" identifies the process by which this guilt is removed and forgiven.

The Goajiro Indians, living on the prong of land which stretches north from Colombia into the Gulf of Mexico, say that forgiveness is "making sin to pass," that is, it passes on and exists no more. The Baouli in the Ivory Coast use a similar phrase in "letting one's sin go," and the Huichols of Mexico say "God takes away one's sin."

The Kpelle people of Liberia speak of forgiveness as "turning one's back on sin." This does not mean, as we might suppose, that a person is despising or rejecting sin, but rather that he refuses to regard the accusation of sin in another. In His forgiveness God refuses to regard our sin. Therefore He turns His back on it. The Barrow Eskimos declare that forgiveness means "from now on to ignore." This means that sin is not to be glossed over, or to be called by another name, but that the one who forgives purposely determines to ignore the sin.

Some expressions for forgiveness may create confusion for us if we do not understand fully their significance. For example, the Navajos speak of forgiveness as "giving a man's sin back to him." This would only seem to heap up guilt and offense. It is not, however, the meaning of the Navajo idiom. Rather, if one sins against another, the offended party possesses a hold upon his soul. But if the offended party "gives his sin back to him," then everything is re-established as it was before the sin was ever committed. The sinner is regarded as completely innocent. This is the mystery of divine forgiveness, whereby God permits forgiven sinners to enter into fellowship with Himself.

In some languages forgiveness is described in terms of the characteristics of the forgiver. The Triques, a small tribe almost hidden away in the mountains of southern Mexico, say that forgiveness consists in "having a big heart." The Tzeltals, farther to the south, say that "God loses our sin in His heart." His heart is so large, and so all-embracing is the magnitude of His love that He "loses our sin in His heart."

Grace

The grace of God explains the mystery of divine forgiveness. The Kissi and Futa-Fula tribes of West Africa speak of grace as simply "goodness." Only goodness could possibly have prompted God's grace toward us. But in general, languages are somewhat more explicit in their definition of grace. For instance, the Tswa people of Southeast Africa, say that grace is "looking with favor upon." This is similar to the San Blas phrase, "God thinks of us for good." This does not mean that there is any essential goodness in man. It is only that God looks upon men as though they were good, regardless of their actual condition. Grace is that attitude which sees the contrite heart beneath the exterior of sin.

In some instances the meaning of "grace" is primarily that which results from the act of bestowing favor. To describe this aspect of grace the Barrow Eskimos say "the help which comes through mercy."

The Totonacs, living on the eastern slopes of the mountains which face toward the Gulf of Mexico, have directed their attention to the response of the recipient of grace. They use the phrase "that which calls for gratitude." Grace is completely undeserved, and hence as a recipient of such unmerited mercy, the soul should be thankful.

Grace, which pervades the entire redemptive process, is regarded from so many points of view. Some people see it as "the goodness of God"; others view it as the act of "looking on with favor"; still others see it as the benefit received, namely, "the help which comes through mercy"; and some see in grace the response of the thankful heart. It is not strange that grace, which is so all-embracing, should be translated in so many ways. Grace is not something which can be seen, handled, measured, and dissected. It is the spiritual fragrance which fills heaven and comes down in mercy over the earth.

Righteousness

Righteousness does not exist outside the plan of God, for it implies conformity to eternal standards. The righteous man is not just "good," but he follows what God has prescribed for men. Goodness tends to be a shifting quality since that which is good is so often defined in purely subjective terms. But that which is righteous implies a divine, nonhuman standard. The Shipibos talk about righteous people as "those who do equal," meaning equal to what men know is right, not necessarily what they regard as simply temporarily good in the sense of good for them. This conformance to a standard is expressed in many languages as a quality of "straightness." The Kabba-Lakas say that the righteous man is "straight straight"—repeating the word to give it positive emphasis. The Zacapoaxtla Aztecs say that a righteous man has a "straight heart," while the Chols, living in southern Mexico, say that the man himself is "straight."

Righteousness is, however, not just behavior. There is a righteousness which men may perform—this is moral righteousness—and a righteousness which men may receive from God—this is imputed or granted righteousness. The latter is "the gift of righteousness" (Romans 5:17), being declared righteous by the grace of God, who sees us as what we can be, and not as what we are. In Barrow Eskimo this righteousness is described as "having sin taken away." It does not mean that people are made perfect, never to do wrong again, but they are made guiltless. This is the only kind of righteousness which sinful mankind could possess, for it likewise is a gift of grace.

Justification

We shy away from such heavy terms as "justification" and "sancti-fication." They seem to be beyond us—theological castles perched upon unscalable heights. Such terms are really only rather awkward ways of speaking about some of the most practical and essential experiences of the Christian faith. The tragedy is that we have set aside the truths which they represent because we have found them too cumbersome to speak about or to grasp.

Justification is that process whereby God makes a man just or righteous. The Zacapoaxtla Aztecs speak of it as "heart-straighten-ing." The Conobs say that it means "having a straight soul." The Popolucas in the state of Veracruz, Mexico, say that this means "walking straight." All of these terms attempt to define the condi-tion which results from justification. The process itself is a little more difficult to describe, but perhaps it can be understood by a phrase used among the Tarascan Indians of Mexico. Let us suppose that a Tarascan father loves his son dearly and admires his outstand-ing qualities, but that this son has a friend who is a person of bad reputation. Nevertheless, this father will gladly receive his son's friend because of love for his own son. To describe this attitude which accepts the friend in the name of the son, the Tarascans use the phrase "he sees him with the goodness of his son." In explaining the Good News about the redemption which we have in Christ, the Tarascan evangelist can point out how there is nothing admirable in us, and yet Christ, the friend of sinners, died for us, and as friends of Christ, we are accepted by God, "who sees us with the goodness of His Son." Justification involves the process of accepting as righteous that which is not in itself righteous, but which is a fit object of mercy because of a truly repentant heart.

There are those who laugh at the doctrine of "justification" and regard it as the fabrication of the theologian's haunted conscience. Quite the contrary! It is the mystery of revealed grace in the lives of the children of God. It lies at the very heart of the gospel, for without justification salvation is not of grace, but of works. But God will not be indebted to any man. It is God who chooses, as illustrated in the Rundi language of Ruanda-Urundi, to "pronounce men guiltless," or as indicated in the Huanuco dialect of Quechua "to hold us as though without sin."

It is felt by some that this type of doctrine leads men to spiritual pride and holier-than-thou bigotry. On the other hand, only a clear perception of the holiness of God, who by grace admits us into His fellowship, sinful as we are, can bring man to the full sense of his own unworthiness. The man who earns his salvation has whereof to boast, but the one who receives it as a free gift is under an eternal constraint to live worthy of the upward calling in Christ Jesus.

Saints

A popular conception is that a saint is one with folded hands and a pious face, who finds his compensation in the claim of being better than other men, who puts off temporal pleasures for the delusion of future rewards, and who in the end is a rather tasteless character, certainly of little good in this world and of questionable value in the next. This idea results from a wrong conception of holiness, for holiness is not the absence of wrong but the presence of goodness. True holiness never seeks retreat from the world, but spends itself in seeking to bring everything under the power and control of God.

In some languages saints are simply called "the children of God." This is not too far from the meaning of the Greek term *hagios*, which implies those who are specially set apart for the service of God. They are the separated ones, not in the Pharisaical sense of being separated from the world, but separated unto holiness. The Zacapoaxtla Aztecs speak of saints as "those with clean hearts," while the Ngok Dinkas call them "those with white hearts." The Conobs describe them by one activity which should characterize their lives, namely, "people of prayer." In one of the Chinese dialects they are called "the holy followers."

Until the Christian church receives a new vision of holiness, as a life of selfless dedication to the will of God, which repudiates the false distinction between the secular and the sacred and seeks to bring all of life into the service of God, men will continue to be confused by the word "saints" and fail to realize that these are just redeemed sinners who have at last found life and have found it more abundantly.

Sanctify

"To sanctify" means literally "to make holy." But this is not the outward holiness of ritual and mumbled prayers in strange languages. It is the holiness of a new life. The Mayas say that sanctification is "making a person clean within." This is not the holiness of the Pharisee, who cleaned the outside of the cup but left the inside filthy (Matthew 23:25). It is the holiness of the soul and heart. The San Blas Indians call it "giving a man a good heart." The Peruvian Huanuco Quechuas say "God perfects us."

It should be noted that this process of sanctifying comes from God. In this, it is similar to all the spiritual experiences of the Christian faith—it is God-derived.

The Kabba-Lakas describe sanctification by a special phrase, "God calls us outside to Himself." This phrase is derived from the practice of a medicine man, who during the initiation rites of apprentices calls upon the young man who is to follow him eventually and to receive all of his secrets and power. From the day that this young man is called out during the height of the ecstatic ceremony, he is identified with his teacher as the heir to his position, authority, and knowledge. The custom, which gives rise to this phrase "call out to himself," illustrates profoundly, though in a limited way, the manner in which the Christian is called out by God to be identified with Him as an heir to the kingdom of heaven, prepared for those who will serve Him.

CHAPTER 11

THUS SAITH
THE LORD

The vocabulary of divine revelation includes not only words of the heart and those of great doctrinal significance, but also terms for the everyday experiences of life—experiences which are described with divine accuracy, for "thus saith the Lord."

Sin

Sin implies standards and reflects the character of the heart. Sin is no accidental act, but the bent of the soul. The Biblical view of sin is much more profound than any current attitudes indicate. This fact is brought out by the words used in various languages to describe the Biblical viewpoint. For example, the Conobs of Guatemala say that sinners are "people with bad hearts." It is not enough to call them "people who do bad things," for though actions do reflect the heart, yet it is the heart with which God is primarily concerned: "For out of the heart proceed evil thoughts, murders, adulteries . . ." (Matthew 15:19). The San Blas people have a more specific word for sinners. They say "people who are doing wrong things in the heart." This is another attempt to describe the subjective character of sin, the kind of sin which Jesus condemned—not the overt deed, but the desire of the evil heart.

Violations of standards also are reflected in words for "sin." The Navajos speak of sin as "that which is off to the side," contrary, that is, to the straight truth. This concept of sin is reflected in the Greek word *paraptóma*, literally "falling to the side of," and is usually translated "transgression." The Greek term *hamartia* means literally "missing the mark." This likewise denotes a standard or goal which has not been attained.

In the Valiente language the term for sin is based upon the end result of sin, namely, "to make oneself guilty."

In some instances a native expression for sin includes many connotations, and its full meaning must be completely understood before one ever attempts to use it. This was true, for example, of the term *hocha* first proposed by Shipibo natives as an equivalent for "sin." The term seemed quite all right until one day the translator heard a girl say after having broken a little pottery jar that she was guilty of *hocha*. Breaking such a little jar scarcely seemed to be sin. However, the Shipibos insisted that *hocha* was really sin, and they explained more fully the meaning of the word. It could be used of breaking a jar, but only if the jar belonged to someone else. *Hocha* was nothing more nor less than destroying the possessions of another, but the meaning did not stop with purely material possessions. In their belief God owns the world and all that is in it. Anyone who destroys the work and plan of God is guilty of *hocha*. Hence the murderer is of all men most guilty of *hocha*, for he has destroyed God's most important possession in the world, namely, man. Any destructive and malevolent spirit is *hocha*, for it is antagonistic and harmful to God's creation. Rather than being a feeble word for some accidental event, this word for sin turned out to be exceedingly rich in meaning and laid a foundation for the full presentation of the redemptive act of God.

Hypocrisy

Of all sins, hypocrisy rated the harshest denunciations by Jesus, for it is above all the sin which destroys and warps the soul. Furthermore, it lends a pretense of religiosity while the life thoroughly reveals the false front of lip service. The duplicity of hypocrisy is described quite similarly in three different Indian languages of

Mexico. The Mixtecos call it "having two heads," the Tzeltals say that a hypocrite is a person with "two hearts," and the Pames declare that a hypocrite has "two mouths."

The Mossi people in French West Africa speak of a hypocrite as "one with a sweet mouth." This is not much different from our own metaphor "honeyed words."

The Piros call a hypocrite "one who just does." This does not mean what it might appear to mean from the English literal translation. It really refers to one who simply acts in accordance with what is convenient without any attention to real motives or desires—thus deeds are separated from character. This represents a subtle kind of hypocrisy which we sometimes overlook. We tend to restrict hypocrisy to actions which are directly designed to cover up the real nature. For the Piros hypocrisy may also be unconscious deeds which are not in keeping with the heart and soul. Hence, the merchant who makes a habit of treating his customers well purely for the sake of business is fundamentally a hypocrite.

Some words for "hypocrite" have interesting legendary backgrounds. For example, in Balinese, it is possible to call a hypocrite a "priest-heron." According to a native legend a heron, intent on catching fish, discovered a lake which was drying up, and he disguised himself as a priest, pretending to be much concerned about the plight of the dying fish. His professed generosity consisted of taking the fish into his long beak with the promise of transporting them to another lake, but they were transported no further than the heron's stomach.

Liar

A liar is a hypocrite of words. The Tarahumaras in northern Mexico call such a person "windy." The Pames, farther to the south, say he is "a much talker." Since in many instances it is hard for a person to be constantly speaking without adding to the truth, they have quite rightly related abundance of speech with distortion of truth.

In the Moré language of West Africa a liar is one who "chops water." Such impossible actions are fitting symbols for fabricated stories.

Pride

Pride is idolatrous self-worship. Arrogance is its priest; greed is its sacrifice; flattery is its ritual. The Shipibos go to the heart of the matter when they describe pride as "declaring 'I outrank others.'" Pride deifies self, even in the guise of humility; it stains the character and leaves the soul untouched by spiritual truth. Pride breaks through in a thousand ways, even in the Sunday-school teacher who finished the lesson about the proud Pharisee and the repentant Publican and then suggested to her class that they all thank God they were not like the Pharisee.

In the Cakchiquel language of Guatemala one speaks of pride as "an unbent neck." Men who insist on holding up their heads in arrogant disdain of others are like the llamas of the altiplano of Peru and Bolivia, which may be tied up with a single rope extending around a herd of twenty or more animals. The rope is attached to the neck of one animal, then drawn around the herd which stand with gawking gaze and stretched necks. It is quite unnecessary to tie the rope separately to each animal, for in their proud attitudes they never lower their heads. They are similar to many people who may be tied by sin simply because they are too proud to bow their heads in repentance. The man who insists on saving his face may lose his life.

Meekness

Not the proud, but "the meek shall inherit the earth." These are the children of the kingdom, for whom God has prepared a place. But meekness is not indolence, nor does it consist in folded hands or wishful thinking. Meekness is a habit of the soul by which men discover life even though they may be robbed of things. The Moré language of West Africa describes the meek man as "one with a shaded heart." His heart is not exposed to the fierce sun of selfish competition; his heart is shaded, and hence his life is cool. The Kipsigis of Kenya, East Africa, describe meekness as "acting slowly." The proud act quickly, for self sees its own interests and is quick to grab its share, but the meek man is not primarily concerned with self. To regard the wishes of others takes slow, deliberate action. In the Kabba-Laka language meekness consists in "having the inner being of a child." Meekness is a gift of humility; pride is the creature of our own sin and self-seeking.

Offend

The word "offend" is used in the New Testament with at least two principal meanings. "If thine eye offend thee" (Mark 9:47) is one kind of offense, but the offense of Matthew 13:21, where people reject the truth because of persecution and tribulation, is quite different.

The first type of offense is described in San Blas as "if your eye spoils your heart." The Greek literally means "to cause to stumble," but this cannot be translated literally in many languages. However, in the San Blas expression we find the truth which the Scriptures teach. It is not a literal stumbling, nor for that matter a literal spoiling of the heart. It is the personality which can be harmed and injured by permitting some part of it to be the instrument or the tool of sin. In the Kipsigis language of Kenya the Greek idiom is very carefully reflected in the phrase "if your eye sets a trap for you." More and more, the eye-appeal may be regarded as the self-appeal, and this must be plucked out if the soul and life are to be preserved.

"Offend" in the sense of "causing to stumble" or "causing to sin" may apply to the relationships among people, as well as within the individual personality. The warning of Mark 9:42 concerning "whosoever shall offend one of these little ones" may be translated in Totonac as "whosoever shall show the wrong road to one of these little ones." By our daily walk we are constantly pointing the way to those who watch us. Every step away from the path which God

would have us walk means that we are showing the wrong road
to someone else. We might be shocked at the very idea of "offend-
ing one of these little ones," and yet when this is put into the language of life as illustrated in the Totonac translation "showing the
wrong road," we are caught up with a jerk and realize that here is
our failure, described in no uncertain terms. For one who is guilty
Jesus said, "it is better that a millstone be hanged about his neck
and he be cast into the sea."

The offense felt by those who reject the truth after they realize
its consequences is described in a number of ways. The Piros say
of those who give up because of fear or lack of interest, "they go by
another road." This does not imply that they arrive at the same
goal. They simply turn off and leave the rest, making their own
trail to suit their own fancies. The Navajos say bluntly "they throw
it away." After having examined the truth, they reject it. The
Kabba-Lakas describe the emotional state of a person who has accepted something and then goes back on it by saying "his soul gets
sick." This is a fit description of the people who followed Jesus for
the loaves and fishes but could not accept the difficult words of
John 6. They were sick in their souls.

The Lomas of Liberia, as noted on page 122, describe faith and
belief as "putting one's hand on it," that is, identifying oneself with
the object of faith. Accordingly, the person who is offended "takes
his hand from it quickly." People who were offended with Jesus did
not care to be identified any longer with him.

Denial of Self

Of all the sayings of Jesus, one seems to stand out pre-eminently
in its power to probe the depths of the soul more acutely than any
other. "If any man would be my disciple, let him deny himself, take
up his cross, and follow me." This threefold challenge to selflessness,
identification, and discipleship expresses in such simple words the
progress of the Christian pilgrim. Denial of self is no common
experience, certainly not apart from the Christian faith; and so it is

not strange that this expression is very difficult to translate. There are no accepted idioms in most languages, for people do not have words for totally alien ideas, and to most people the denial of self is as foreign as anything could be.

The Zoque Indians of southern Mexico describe the denial of self as simply "forgetting self," while the Mazatecs, farther to the north, speak of it as "covering up self." The Aztecs of Tetelcingo, Mexico, say that to deny oneself is literally "not to accept self." Each of these phrases points to the rejection or elimination of self. The Pame Indians are more specific. They declare that a person must "not do what he himself wants to do." This comes closer to the center of the psychological problem and is paralleled by the Tzeltal idiom "stop doing what your heart wants."

The denial of self does not consist in denying oneself the things of life, but rather in denying the desires of the ego, which constitute life for the self-centered soul. The Huanuco Quechuas translate the denial of self as "to declare, 'I do not live for myself.'" Translated in this way with the pronouns "I . . . myself," it reflects vividly the experience of anyone who has come to the point in his Christian life where he finally realizes the ultimate challenge which Christ makes to the whole of life. Denying self does not imply death. Rather it means living for someone else; and for the Christian this means living for Christ. In the words of Paul, "For me to live is Christ." This is the positive aspect of denying self.

In the Loma language the truth of denying self is expressed somewhat differently by the phrase "to take his mind out of himself." This means that one is not to be constantly concerned about self, seeking one's own interests and being dominated by selfish motives. This "taking of the mind out of self" is precisely what psychotherapists have been telling all kinds of neurotics, whose introspection is an ever-narrowing whirl of increased velocity until the soul is prostrated by its self-induced dizziness. The cure for this is a denial of self, following the Loma formula of "taking one's mind out of self."

Confession

Confession cleanses the soul, not by virtue of its psychological "ventilation," but because the penetrating light of the Spirit of God discovers the hidden recesses of the heart and exposes the secret self, so that we can become integrated personalities. The Pames speak of confession as "pulling out the heart" that it may be clearly seen—not just by men, but by God. Confession may be called merely "telling the truth" or "admitting one's guilt," but true confession goes far beyond that. It is the exposure of the life to the curative influences of self-exposed living.

The verb "confess" is not used, however, exclusively in connection with sin, for in Luke 12:8 one "confesses the Lord." The Gbeapo people of Liberia speak of this as "talking His good name." This means not only a formal declaration of allegiance, which people may make in church, but making it a habit to talk about the good name of the Lord. This type of confession implies something much more profound than the artificial declarations that some people make in certain moments of emotional excitement. The living reality of the faithful conversation determines both the nature and the reality of confession.

Communion

Where sin has raised a wall, confession pierces the barrier, and communion restores the fellowship. Communion is essentially the experience of friendship, and it has both a giving and receiving aspect. The Zoques of southern Mexico speak of communion as "the act of being and having a friend." Reciprocity is the very essence of communion. The neighboring Tzeltal people speak of communion simply as "being companions one with another."

One of the features of communion is the exchange of ideas. Communion is not proximity, for in the densest crowds there may be the loneliest souls. Communion implies common interests, and the greater the number of these points of common interest, the greater is the communion. When at last all differences are resolved, perfect communion may result. The Mazatecs of Mexico describe this type of communion in the expression "the two are dovetailed," a figure of speech derived from the process of joining pieces of wood together by dovetailing the respective parts. A perfect fit is the prerequisite for perfect communion.

The importance of time and the exchange of ideas in communion is interestingly brought out in the Zapotec dialect of Mitla, Mexico, where communion is described as "boiling words." This figure of speech does not imply any hot discussions or heated arguments, but it is a picture of the bubbling pot on the fire, typifying the cheery talk of people who sit long hours chatting about their common hopes, ambitions, and desires. Communion with God is not the cataclysmic leap of the soul into the spiritual unknown. Rather it is the result of hours spent with Him, talking about the most personal, intimate, and practical details of life. Communion is not a dash toward security, but a walk toward reality, with our hands in His.

The Karré people of Equatorial Africa have expressed this truth by the words "to push our feet ahead together"—walking together against obstacles, but together.

Discipleship

Discipleship is one kind of communion, for our Teacher is not one who lectures to, but who speaks with, the needy soul. The Kipsigis of Kenya call a disciple an "apprentice." When a noted medicine man becomes old, there are many young men who vie with one another to become his apprentice, seeking to learn his secrets and to inherit his sacred bundles of fetishes and charms. They wish to learn to be like their teacher, and to do this they must associate with him, watch his actions, note his magic techniques, and see how he deals with his patients. The Christian disciple must undergo a similar period of training if he is to be a real disciple of the Master. Disciples are more than "learners" or "students." They are "imitators

of the teacher," as the Zacapoaxtla dialect of Aztec expresses it. But
even in the process of learning, they are not passive receivers of
knowledge—they are, as the Valientes say, "truth searchers."

Marvel

To marvel is one of the first experiences of the true disciple. But
to express this emotional attitude is not always easy, for languages
employ so many different ways of describing what seems to us such
a self-evident kind of emotion. The Kekchis say that "to marvel" is
literally "to lose one's heart." In one's amazement the heart seems
to disappear completely. The Tzeltals describe this experience even
more vividly by the words "he felt like dying." We might speak of
"dying" from fright, or wishing we could die in cases of great embar-
rassment, but we would not think of dying from amazement.

The Tarascans in central Mexico describe astonishment as "to shut
one's mouth, thinking." One is so overwhelmed with thoughts that
there is nothing to say. The Mixtecos, farther to the south, talk about
"marveling" in quite a different way. They say "to forget, listening."
That is, the report is so marvelous that it makes one completely
forget everything else.

In the Loma language the report of Jesus' astonishment at the unbelief of the people (Mark 6:6) is expressed as "their unbelief was
so great that his mind walked away." His thoughts simply could not
endure the willful unbelief of the multitude.

Persuasion

For many of us "persuasion" means a kind of high-pressure im-
position of one man's ideas upon another. The Greek term for "persuasion," however, implies more the idea of creating confidence. The
phrase used by the Conobs is even more personal and intimate in its
implications. It is literally "to give one's soul to." If someone per-
suades another, he figuratively "gives his soul to him." Real, lasting,
and effective persuasion must involve this giving process. Thus it is

in direct conflict with modern propaganda which imposes itself on the mind. The persuasion of the Scriptures gives itself to the heart and soul.

Prayer

It is an easy mistake for the missionary translator to substitute for "prayer" some word for "reciting" or "chanting," since in the understanding of so many peoples in the world prayer is a kind of mechanical mumbling of strange sounds—a religious "hocus-pocus dominocus" essentially similar to the extravagant and weird cries of animists pleading with their spirit gods and thinking that they are heard because of their "much speaking" (Matthew 6:7). In order to teach the true meaning of prayer, the translator frequently uses the phrase "to talk with God."

There are millions of people in the world who have never thought of "talking to God." Rather they pray to idols or saints, spirits or demons—anything, provided they think that their words may finally reach some supernatural power which can and will help them. But to talk to God seems incredible and quite impossible.

Some translators have unwittingly tended to make spiritual beggars of Christians by using a word for prayer which means "to beg for." The Tzotzils employ the verb "to ask for" as a part of their phrase for prayer, but they add "with the heart coming out." This rules out selfish praying, for asking with the heart out leaves no place for self to hide.

Increase and Decrease

The translation of John 3:30, "He must increase, but I must decrease," is not easy. These words can be reproduced in other languages, but the meaning may be purely physical, not spiritual. When the translators among the Mazatecs in Mexico asked their informants for words to translate this verse, they were given the expressions "to get big" and "to get small." But these phrases had no meaning other than physical size. They tried again and got the words "to get tall" and "to get short," but these terms were no more satisfactory. They tried still another time and received "to get huge" and "to get puny." Always there was the same difficulty—the words had only the connotation of size, and never the idea of importance. Finally, in desperation they said to their informants, "But the verse doesn't mean just size, it means that one person must be more important, and the other less important."

"Oh then," their helpers replied, "why didn't you tell us? We say, 'He must be more of a chief, and I must be more of a follower.'" This is the contrast which describes true discipleship.

The Shilluks of the Anglo-Egyptian Sudan express this all-important development in the Christian life as, "He must come in out of the morning, and I must go out into the night." Christ must come in out of the misty dawn of our own neglect to take His rightful place of Lordship, while the life of self must recede and be lost in the night of selflessness.

Lord

Terms which are used to translate "Lord" focus attention on many aspects of His relationship to men and theirs to Him. The Valientes call the Lord "a place double man," that is, one who takes the place of two men, in the sense that He is greater than other men. To the San Blas people such a term would seem inadequate, for they say "the great one above all."

The Amuesha Indians of Peru describe the Lord as "one who carries us." This is the sustaining and keeping relationship of the Lord to His people. In several languages of Liberia the Lord is spoken of as "a person-owner." But this is not used in reference to some chief who owns slaves. Its meaning goes much deeper. Before one can be "an owner of a person," he must have "redeemed" such a person. And in this lies the essence of the gospel. Christ becomes our Lord because He is our Redeemer, our Owner. Redemption calls for lordship, and lordship requires obedience.

God

It is sometimes rather difficult to find an adequate term for "God" because people have such a hazy idea about Him. They may think of Him as some indefinite and remote person, but their primary concern is about the evil spirits which do them harm. They would rather spend their time and energies placating their enemies than entreating God, in whom they have little or no confidence.

In some instances the native term for God is excellent. For example, the Mbanza people of northern Congo believe in Chuchu and they claim that he made the world and mankind. What is more, he likes mankind. But his people did not like him. To escape from him, they ran away and have practically forgotten about him, though he has never forgotten about them. Here, embedded in the legends of the people, lies the truth which the missionary may use. He may show the people how far they have wandered from God and how He has not forgotten about them. In fact, He sent His Son in order that He might reconcile them to Himself.

To the San Blas people God is "our Great Father." This is the phrase which they themselves have used for God, and though it emphasizes but one aspect of God, it is one of the most important. The Chanca Quechuas of Peru speak of God as "the One who is sufficient"—sufficient for all things, including rebellious mankind.

In the Kipsigis language the word for God is *Jehoba*, which looks very much indeed like English "Jehovah." But it is not a borrowing from English. This Kipsigis word actually means "the Great Ruler," and it is the traditional Kipsigis word for God.

Once a missionary has found a word for "God" and another for "son," it would seem only natural that the phrase "Son of God" would be extremely easy to use. This is true, even in the Tarahumara language of northern Mexico, but these proud and reserved people understand the phrase only as a name for a Tarahumara Indian. They regard themselves as "sons of God," while all foreigners are "sons of the devil." In some aspects of racial pride they far outdistance the Anglo-Saxons. The basic difference is that they do not propagandize the idea, for their superiority is so fully accepted among them that they regard its truth as self-evident. In the translation of the New Testament into the Tarahumara language, Christ must be spoken of as "the only Son of God," unless one wishes to imply that Jesus was just another Tarahumara Indian.

Respecter of Persons

The meaning of the phrase "no respecter of persons" is so obvious to us that we tend to forget the fact that the real meaning is almost hidden behind the bare words. In one sense God does respect people, for He respects human personality; but He does not respect persons in the sense of choosing people because of their outward appearance or their private claims to recognition. In order to translate Ephesians 6:9 "neither is there respect of persons with Him," the Zoque translation in Mexico reads, "He does not pick people out on sight." That is, God does not regard external appearance, but He sees the heart. The Cashibos in Peru say, "He doesn't just look at the face," for though the face may tell a long story, it can still hide an evil heart.

A related statement made to Jesus by the accusing Pharisees, "Thou regardest not the person of men" (Mark 12:14), must be variously rendered, for often this expression does not permit a literal translation. The Shipibo translation reads, "In your mind no one is anything." Literally, of course, this is not true, but it is an idiom in Shipibo which most strikingly declares the truth of this passage, for Jesus did not fawn before the religious leaders of His day nor seek the prestige of the rabbinical schools. He declared His message without favor. To describe this kind of bold pronouncement of judgment and truth, the Kipsigis say bluntly, "to declare truth without bribes." Where, as is so common in native courts, so-called justice is for sale to the highest bidder, "one who declares truth without bribes" is indeed a fit description of one who regards not the person of a man but the truth of God.

Glory

It is sometimes easier to find a name for God than to discover adequate terms for some of His attributes. One of these difficult words is "glory." Where people have kings, to whom they give honor, pomp, and majesty, it is not too hard to find some word roughly equivalent to "glory," even though at first it is weak in meaning and must acquire its rich connotations from its usage in Scripture. However, there are some tribes of people who seem to have nothing even remotely resembling "glory" in the sense of an attribute of personality. How is this concept to be developed?

In the Navajo language the word for glory means "what shines out." Hence, God's glory is the shining character of His presence and personality. The Maya language makes this more specific by speaking of God's glory as "the beauty of God." In the San Blas language it is "the reflection of strong brightness."

If a term for "glory" is difficult to find, then an adequate expression for "glorify" is often ten times harder to discover. The process by which God glorifies us is usually more easily translated than the way in which we may glorify Him. His glorifying us can be translated as "He imparts brightness to us." But there is no way in which we can impart brightness to Him, for He is the very source of this glory. In the Kpelle language of Liberia one can say "to lift up God's brightness." This means to exalt His brightness before men by praising His works and recounting His wonderful deeds unto the children of men. The Shipibos declare that to glorify God means "to brag about God." This may strike some at first as being an unspiritual approach, but it surely is Pauline, for Paul used the word "to brag" when he declared his confidence in Jesus Christ and in the salvation of the world which God wrought through His Son. The tragedy of our churches today is that we do brag—though perhaps in subtle ways—about our denominations, our buildings, our attendance, and our programs—about everything except Him who is the author and finisher of our faith.

Worship

Worship is the response of the soul overwhelmed by the glory of God. The Valiente Indians describe the heart which prostrates itself in worship as "cutting itself down before God." This figure of speech comes from the picture of towering mahoganies in the forest which, under the woodman's ax, quiver, waver, and then in solemn, thunderous crashing bury their lofty heads in the upstretched arms of the surrounding forest. This is the experience of every true worshiper who sees "the Lord, high and lifted up." Our own unworthiness brings us low. As the Valientes say, "we cut ourselves down before" His presence. Our heads, which have been carried high in self-confidence, sink lower and lower in worship. The Tzeltals have a very similar expression. They say that worship consists in "ending oneself before God." Only by coming to the end of oneself can one truly worship. The animist worships his deities in the hope of receiving corresponding benefits, and some pagans in Christendom think that church attendance is a guarantee of success in this life and good luck in the future. But God has never set a price on worship except the price that we must pay, namely, "coming to the end of ourselves."

At the same time, there is a positive aspect of worship which goes beyond the subjective consciousness that God is all and in all. It is the worship of praise and thanksgiving—what the Kpelles of Liberia call "raising up a blessing unto the Lord."

The Comforter

As we noted on page 20, perhaps no word in all the New Testament is so hard to translate adequately as the word "Comforter" (John 14:16). The Greek word, generally transliterated as *Paraclete*, is exceedingly rich in its wealth of meaning, for it implies not only "to comfort" but also "to admonish," "to exhort," "to encourage," and "to help." To put all these meanings into one native expression is indeed difficult, and yet the missionary translator must try to find a term or phrase which will give the people an adequate picture of the unique ministry of the Holy Spirit.

In the Joloano Moro language of southern Philippines the people use the phrase "the one who goes alongside continuously." In this sense He is the constant companion of the believer. In one of the Otomi Indian dialects in central Mexico the native believers have suggested the phrase "He who gives warmth in our soul." One can readily see the picture of the chilled heart and life seeking comfort in the Living Word and finding in the ministry of the Spirit of God that warmth which the soul so needs if it has to live in the freezing atmosphere of sin and worldly cares.

The Baouli Christians speak of the Comforter as "He who ties up the thoughts." The thoughts of the worried heart are scattered every place in senseless and tormenting disorder. The Comforter ties up these distracted thoughts, and though they still exist, they are under the control of the Spirit. We cannot rid ourselves of worry by denying our thoughts or by hoping that through some psychotherapeutic magic we can forget them. What we need is to have them under control, "tied up," as the Baouli say. Then we can experience the joy of inner peace: "Thou wilt keep him in perfect peace whose mind is stayed on Thee."

CHAPTER 12

THE WORD SPEAKS
TO THE PEOPLE

Translation of the Bible is not enough. It must be in the hands of the people if the Spirit of God is to speak to them. The translations which have been published by the missionaries or Bible Societies are often distributed by the missionary translators themselves, who may journey for weeks through scattered villages in remote mountain valleys or along winding jungle streams to bring to men the message which they can read and study for themselves. The missionary must frequently engage in literacy campaigns and set up schools or arrange for evening classes around the village fire. Thus eyes and minds unaccustomed to strange symbols on paper may have an entire new world opened to them.

The Scriptures are also distributed by colporteurs, consecrated men who dedicate themselves to the task of selling the Word of God in villages and hamlets, along dusty roads and in busy harbors, on crowded street corners and in noisy markets—anywhere that men can be reached with the Truth. Generally the Scriptures are sold, not primarily for the sake of the money, for the price rarely covers the cost of publication. But selling the Scriptures, even at a loss, has two principal advantages. First, the one who buys appreciates the book immeasurably more than if it were given, and secondly, the colporteur has a wonderful opportunity to speak extensively with his customers in order to persuade them of the importance of the Book and their need of the message. There are times in which great value may be derived from a planned campaign of free distribution, but too often free books are unwanted books, and they are likely to be regarded as political propaganda. By selling the books for a few cents, or even in exchange for some eggs, salt, a little piece of meat, or lodging for the night, the colporteur has the opportunity to witness concerning his own faith in this message from God and to plant in the hearts of his hearers a desire to know more of what God has said. A few cents invested in a book is usually a guarantee that the book will be read. And if men read, the Spirit speaks.

The name "colporteur" which is given to "Bible peddlers" is not a new term. The Oxford Dictionary lists it as being in use as early as 1796. It is borrowed from French *colporteur* and means literally "one who carries (*porter*) from the neck (*col*)." The modern colporteur may carry his books in a suitcase, a knapsack, a blanket roll, saddlebags, or a small trunk; and he may travel afoot, by car, bus, train, boat, canoe, camel, donkey, or plane. He is the man with the Book, in search of the spiritually needy man without the Book.

What would ever prompt a person to give up the relative comforts of home and friends to make long journeys among unfriendly people to sell a Book which many despise? Only the constraining love of Christ and the sustaining work of the Spirit of God can produce real colporteurs. One such man was Vicente Quiroga, who in 1878, at the time of a violent earthquake in northern Chile, was stationed to guard a beach littered with rubble from boats which had been wrecked by a giant tidal wave. Among the shattered boxes, crates, and broken spars, he noticed a few pages of a strange book. After drying them out in the hot sun, he read them. They contained the strangest message he had ever heard, but he could not understand what it was all about. Several times he read over the pages, and each time he became more fascinated, but more confused. At last he asked a friend to look at the pages, and this friend suggested that they might come from a book called the Bible. After many weeks Vicente Quiroga finally found a missionary, and from him he obtained a Bible. At last he could read all of the message, and it entered his heart and soul. Within a short time he dedicated himself to the task of taking this Book to the small villages along the scant streams of the desert of northern Chile. At the end of twenty years there was scarcely a hamlet or a home in all that part of Chile which had not received a call from this humble colporteur, who had found in the Book of life the message of life for dying people.

The man who distributes the Bible to Bibleless people is also a witness to its message. A few of the questions often asked by the Hindus of India are:

"When and why did you become a Christian?"

"In what way is your religion different from ours?"

"Why do you seek to convert people of other faiths?"

"In what way is your Bible superior to our Vedas, Citas, and Upanishads?"

"There have been many saints in India and elsewhere; why do you give a unique position to Christ?"

"Why cannot one remain a Hindu and practice Christianity?"

Unless the representative of God's Word has learned in humility the Divine uniqueness of John 14:6, "I am the way, the truth, and the life; no one comes to the Father, but by me," he cannot answer the taunts of enemies or the earnest inquiries of searching souls.

Colporteurs, missionaries, and evangelists in India have spread the Word of God and the knowledge of Jesus Christ to an extent which is surprising to many. At the death of Gandhi the Hindu newspapers, in attempting to praise him, frequently likened him to Christ and never to any Hindu deity. This fact alone should make one realize the extent to which the message of the Book has entered the thinking of many even though as yet it may not have won their personal allegiance.

So great has been the influence of the Bible in some parts of the Mohammedan world that one leading Moslem newspaper in Teheran, Iran, recently declared, "The Iranian Constitution is the Gospel of democracy and the Bible of liberty." What they do not realize as yet is that there is no abiding democracy or true liberty apart from the message of spiritual equality, which makes each man personally accountable to God through the grace of Jesus Christ. In Mohammedan areas the Bible has an even more strategic ministry than in many parts of the world, for religious fanaticism often severely restricts the ministry of a missionary, but it is not sufficient to keep out the Book. The result is that in scores of homes in such cities as Khartoum and Omdurman in the Anglo-Egyptian Sudan devoted Bible women teach the Word of God to women whose seclusion keeps them from any contacts with a Christian congregation.

The Bible not only has a message for the isolated women of the Mohammedan household, but it also speaks to those unfortunate victims of vice. One colporteur in Syria was chatting with a converted watchmaker when two gaudily-dressed women came in with a watch for repair. One of them used a couple of words of Turkish, and the colporteur was quick to speak to her in that language. She proved to be a Greek from Istanbul, and so she was offered a Gospel in Modern Greek. "Not that Book," she protested. "Not in that cursed house where I work." Only then did the colporteur know her profession. "Take it," he urged. "I too was a sinner until I took this Book and learned that Jesus was willing to take all my sins upon Himself." The women departed to their near-by quarters, but in a short time they returned with eight others, each asking for a copy of the Book with its message of grace and forgiveness for those who had been tied by a cruel fate to such a slavery.

The spread of the message in China was discouragingly slow. Robert Morrison, whose pioneer translation was accomplished in spite of so many serious obstacles (see pages 97-99), could count only ten believers after twenty-five long years of tireless work. But within a century distribution of the Scriptures reached a total figure of 13,921,461 Bibles, Testaments, and portions in one year. Colportage in China has so frequently faced stern opposition and fanatical persecution that Bible distributors have learned to suffer. One evangelist colporteur in Shantung had led thousands of people to a knowledge of Christ and remained at his post after the Communists took over. A short time later he and a friend were seized and put into prison. They were questioned as to why, in these enlightened days, they still preached an out-of-date doctrine like Christianity. Was it because they wanted money, or were they in the employ of some American agency? The colporteur's simple witness to the gospel message was followed by a severe beating and torture on the "wheel." Suddenly and unaccountably released, he hobbled north to Hopei province and the Bible House, to continue his humble ministry of introducing men to the Living Word, revealed in the written Word.

This Book has not been stopped by political boundaries, and the picture in China has been filled with strange contradictions. One Bible Society representative in Hankow reported:

Another time I met a Communist political officer (they are strictly forbidden to have religion) hesitatingly talking about the question of God in the house of one of my friends. He brought out a small New Testament from inside his uniform and showed it to me. On the frontispiece, in very beautiful Chinese characters, had been written: "This is the most precious present given to me by my mother, and I must keep it in my bosom forever." He told me, "Whenever there is no one about, I open my Testament, read, and weep without restraint."

There are times when the Church seems to face extinction in some parts of the world. The tiny Christian community of Kashgar, East Turkestan, numbered several hundred persons in 1933, but Moslem opposition, combined with Russian domination, resulted in the martyrdom of the young leader, Muhammed Abel Akhond, and in the scattering of the believers as well as the violent expulsion of the missionaries from the land. But the New Testament in the language of the people was sent back as "a missionary without passport."

The story of the Word alone in the hands of national believers is an indisputable testimony to the work of the Holy Spirit as He guides, inspires, and advances the work of the church. The Japanese rulers of Formosa had always had difficult dealings with the aboriginal tribes in the mountains. Finally, a peace negotiated by a remarkable Tyal woman named Chi-oang brought police stations and schools to the Tyal villages, but it did not prevent head-hunting—it only meant that Japanese heads were preferred. The Japanese tried to impose Shintoism on the aborigines and strictly prohibited the work of missionaries among them.

In 1929 Chi-oang, who had become a Christian, was persuaded to go to Bible school for two years. She felt quite incapable of doing anything, for she regarded herself as quite an old woman. However, upon her return to the villages on the east coast, she began to teach her Tyal people in small groups, often at night because of official persecution. But despite the efforts of the Japanese police, who had outlawed the movement, people came to hear the message of God's redeeming love in Christ Jesus.

A Tyal young man named Dowai also obtained Bible training and went to work among his people, distributing Bibles in Japanese, for the school system had succeeded in teaching Japanese to many of the young people. The police tried to burn all the Bibles; and failing in this, they arrested Dowai. In the midst of this persecution World War II came, and in desperation the Japanese police did all they could to stamp out the church. The church program was always the same: weeks of secret indoctrination until the convert was fully grounded in the faith, and then the commission to go and win others. Though Tyal Christians were imprisoned, beaten, threatened, and killed, the message taught by this humble old woman Chi-oang stood the test. When the war was over and the church was permitted to come out into the open, there was a Christian community of more than four thousand members.

Nations which reject the Bible have always had to reckon with the claims of God. In the early days of attempted missionary work in Japan, the emperor pronounced the edict:

So long as the sun shall warm the earth, let no Christian be so bold as to come to Japan; and let all know that the King of Spain himself or the Christians' God or the great God of All, if he violate this command, shall pay for it with his head.

Not only has the message of the Bible entered Japan, but during the first five years after World War II more than five million New Testaments and Bibles were distributed in Japan, and the Christian leaders asked for ten million copies more for distribution within a three-year period—so great was the demand for the Word of God among the people who lost their god on a single day. The Japanese religious system, so carefully developed through the centuries, seemed to have collapsed almost overnight when the emperor, who was regarded as the divine link between humanity and the heavenly deity, declared himself no longer god. It is little wonder that people who had lost a war, lost an empire, and lost a god wanted to know about the message of Jesus Christ.

Perhaps no church in the Orient has a more remarkable story than the Batak congregations of Sumatra. Dr. Nommensen of the Rhenish Missionary Society approached the Batak chief in 1864 and asked for permission to live among his people for two years. At the end of that time the chief thanked him for all he had done, but said that it was now time for him to go because everything that he had taught was contained in their own tribal laws. "We likewise have laws saying, 'Thou shalt not kill; thou shalt not steal; thou shalt not commit adultery.' You have said nothing that we did not already know."

Dr. Nommensen had been so concerned about the low ethical standards of the people that he had concentrated all of his attention on the divine prohibitions, which, however, had failed to arouse moral conviction within the hearts of the Batak people. He determined to cease stressing the need for moral laws and to proclaim the saving power of Christ. He pleaded with the chief to permit him to stay just six months more. At the end of this time the chief came to him again saying, "In these last months you have told us something new. We now realize that we cannot even keep our own laws, but we want Jesus Christ as our Lord."

Thousands accepted the Saviour, and there is now a Christian community of more than one hundred thousand people distributed among eight hundred churches, served by fifty-five ordained ministers and a vast number of lay leaders. The Bible, translated into the Batak language by one of the great scholars sent out in the early days by the Netherlands Bible Society, has been the foundation of this unparalleled development. Many of the neighboring Moslems have been so impressed by the peaceful prosperity of the Christian communities that they have asked permission to come and live within their boundaries. This is the message of the Kingdom, being spontaneously expressed in the community life of converted men and women.

Africa is the awakening continent, where more rapid strides are being made toward literacy than in any other area in the world. Plans made in 1944 for British colonies envisage forty million new literates within thirty years' time. Similar programs are being conducted in French, Belgian, and independent areas. Everywhere in the dark continent the people are awakening. In this process they are revolting against tribal backwardness, imperialistic practices, economic enslavement, and social discrimination. There are some who strike out blindly against real or imagined enemies, but there are others who are pleading for more copies of the Scriptures. One missionary in Ruanda-Urundi has asked, "What can I do? I received as my allotment of Scriptures only forty New Testaments, and there are four thousand Ruanda people in my area asking me for copies of the Word of God." In scattered jungle villages, in mining compounds, and along desert caravan trails the Word of God is needed in Africa. At least some parts of the Scriptures have been translated into more than 350 African languages and dialects, but there are at least 300 more languages (though these are relatively small) in which there is nothing.

Even when there have been no Bible vans, bookstores, or mission stations with supplies of Scriptures, there have been Africans who have felt the call of God to distribute the Word. Chiwale, an Umbundu of Angola, was taken off by the Portuguese to forced labor on the island of São Thomé in the Gulf of Guinea, but he carried with him a hymn book, the Gospels, and Acts. At night by the light of a small fire in the laborers' compound, he copied off on cheap blue paper the message of the Word and distributed it to his companions. It was crudely done, but it was the message of new life. When these men returned to their village homes, this humble ministry resulted in more than sixty congregations.

The Bible has spoken to Africans because, as in all languages, it speaks to the heart. One little Chiluba schoolboy in Congo listened attentively to the reading of the Scriptures and immediately afterward went to the missionary, asking to borrow that Book. He wanted to take it back with him into the jungle to read to his parents in the distant village, "For those words made holes in my heart." The penetrating voice of the Spirit of God is speaking to hundreds of thousands of Africans today.

In Latin America the colporteur suffers the hostility of enforced ignorance imposed by the long shadows of the Inquisition. The Bible is often an unknown Book. One colporteur in Peru went down into the jungle towns and villages to preach and distribute the Word. A policeman tried to stop him; but failing in this, he arrested and dragged him off to the police station. The colporteur explained to the sergeant his reasons for being there and told him the story of the Good Shepherd seeking the lost sheep. The sergeant listened thoughtfully, and then replied, "Yes, I myself am that lost sheep."

Many colporteurs in Latin America sell primarily in the market places. Like Enrique Bazan in Oruro, a busy town almost 13,000 feet high in the mountain plateau of Bolivia, they set up little tables with books, display posters with attractive pictures, and then begin to tell curious crowds about the most important Book in the world. In the busy market, filled with noisy merchants and haggling buyers, they endeavor to sell Gospels primarily, for almost any person will spend a few cents to buy a small book, while most people are rather cautious about buying an entire book, especially one which is so often spoken against. It is the policy of the Bible

Societies to encourage the sale of Gospels and other portions in order that the seed may be planted in otherwise unreached hearts. Colporteurs who sell only Bibles are likely to be reaching only the Christians, but the Gospels reach the great unevangelized multitudes.

Fanaticism, fostered by ignorance, blinds men to truth. Valentin Dorantes, a colporteur in Morelos, Mexico, was invited to the house of a man who had promised to buy some Bibles. But on entering the house, he was taken to an open grave which two men had just finished digging. He was told that his body would be thrown into it after being filled with bullets, for he was guilty of "distributing false books."

"No, they are not false," Valentin Dorantes insisted. "They are the Good News. And God has permitted me to be brought here in order that you may know what God has said. You may kill me, but you will not be able to say in the judgment that no one has ever told you that Christ is the only one by whom we can be saved."

Then Dorantes asked his intended murderer for permission to read just a small portion of this Book which was supposed to be so false. Since it is customary in Mexico to give to a person who is about to die a chance to say a few last words, he was granted this opportunity. He began to read the third chapter of John and stopped to explain briefly the meaning of John 3:16 and to mention the love which would prompt God to send His Son to such a sinful world. One of the men then asked, "What is this love, anyway?" "If you will permit me, I will read what this Book says about 'love,'" Dorantes replied. He turned then to I Corinthians 13. He had scarcely finished reading and commenting briefly on the love of God when the daughter in the family began to cry and to plead with her mother to prevent the death of a man who had read such beautiful words.

The mother turned to the colporteur and urged him to go on reading from that Book, which none of them had ever heard before. Dorantes continued, and his would-be murderer shoved his pistol back into its holster and wiped his eyes, which were beginning to betray the conviction which was entering his soul. After a few minutes he interrupted the colporteur, "Have no more fear! Come into the house and tell us more! I had been deceived; I did not know the truth about that Book."

The Word of God must go not only to unevangelized men and women in remote hamlets and villages but to those who sail the sea and turn up in strange ports in need of the Bread of Life. A colporteur in Port Said on the Red Sea visits the ships which come into the harbor. In one month he boarded 114 ships, under twenty-two different flags, and sold Scriptures in twenty-six different languages. On a ship flying the flag of Panama, he was challenged by the second mate to produce a Bible in his language, Estonian. The colporteur did have a Bible in Estonian, and the surprised officer readily bought it.

At one port in the Near East, Colporteur Towfic was selling Scriptures to some stevedores as they were lunching on bread and melons, when suddenly the British captain bore down on the group and demanded to know what Towfic was doing there. In his broken English he tried to explain that he was selling the Bible.

"Are you an evangelist?" the captain demanded.

"Yes, I am the littlest servant of everybody. Please, Sir, you buy Bible, too?"

The captain shouted his refusal, but the colporteur politely and earnestly urged him and thrust a copy of the New Testament into his pocket. The captain stopped for a moment, and then took Towfic inside. Instead of the rough handling which the colporteur expected, he found himself sitting down to a cup of tea with the captain who was asking him about religion. "Do you sell the Koran as well?" the captain inquired.

"No. Jesus Messiah enough for you, enough for me," was his simple answer from a heart of faith.

There is a special group of people who must have the Scriptures prepared in a special way. These are the blind. Already there are Scriptures for them in more than fifty languages. And perhaps more than any other group in the world they have found light in the Word. On one occasion the writer was preaching in a small church in southern Mexico. Near the rear door sat a white-haired woman whose face shone with the radiance of joy and whose presence seemed to bless the entire congregation. Tepoxina Cordova was blind, but she had seen more of the truth than the others. As we parted she said, "The reading of the Bible is my life." Those wrinkled hands, gliding over the raised points of the Bible in Spanish Braille, had brought the spiritual light of the Word to a life in physical darkness.

Blind people not only receive the Word, they also distribute it. Guadalupe Rosillo, a blind woman in Mexico City, has for many years visited the homes of those to whom the Bible is a strange or forbidden book. Her humble sweetness and joyful witness have stood out in bold contrast to the professional beggars who ask for money in the name of religious charity. She does not ask for help but offers to all the help of the Son of God.

Some books are bought and thrown away, but even some of these get into the hands of earnest seekers. Turribio Torrejon was rummaging through the dump heaps on the salt flats at the edge of Oruro, Bolivia, when he noticed part of a book. There were only a hundred or so pages, but it was a fascinating book. It contained things about Jesus Christ that he had never heard. He had no idea what this book was, but he kept it and read it.

One day he met an old friend on the train, and as they rode along, the friend began to tell Turribio about what had happened in his life. This friend had found Jesus Christ, and now, instead of being a drunkard, everything was different. In the Bible which he had been reading he had found the truth for which he had looked so long.

"But the Bible is a forbidden book," Turribio Torrejon remonstrated. "You'll be deceived if you read it."

Whereupon, his friend took a Bible out of his suitcase and began to read it, challenging his friend to find anything false in what this Book had to say.

"Oh, but that is not the Bible!" Torrejon insisted. "That is the book I have been reading." Then he pulled out of his traveling basket the carefully preserved leaves of a part of the New Testament. Immediately he began to compare the words, the chapters, and the books. "Yes, they are the same," he finally admitted. "To think—all this time I have been reading the Bible and did not know it."

His friend then continued to explain more of the message of the forbidden Book. By the time the journey had ended, Turribio Torrejon had given his heart to the Saviour, and the next day he sought out a missionary from whom he could obtain a complete Bible and learn more of its message of salvation.

The need of the Word is not limited to Asia, Africa, and Latin America. In so-called Christian lands this same truth is life to dying men. During World War II a young Belgian parachutist was dropped into his country to work with the underground movement against the Germans. He was captured by the Gestapo and placed in solitary confinement. In the cell at his side was a Belgian pastor, likewise accused of espionage. These men discovered that they could communicate with each other by tapping the Morse code on the intervening wall. On one occasion the parachutist tapped, "It is hell to be alone with oneself." To this the pastor replied, "It is heaven to be alone with one's Lord."

Sensing the parachutist's deep spiritual need, the pastor arranged with members of his congregation on the outside to send a Bible to this young man. But it was not merely a Bible which came into this young man's cell. Jesus Christ came into his life and transformed it there in his solitary confinement. So much so that on his way to his execution he tapped out slowly to the Belgian pastor, who was later released, "I am going out to life and not to death."

The Bible is the message of life because it reveals the Living Christ who gave His life that we might live. This is the Book which must be translated, published, distributed, and read in all the languages of earth.

SCRIPTURAL INDEX

LANGUAGE INDEX

GENERAL INDEX

"Adam's apple," 52
Africa, 17, 29, 34, 45, 172
agapaô, 63
agapê, 125
"age," 60
Alaska, 125, 140, 144
"alms," 25
Alphabets, difficult ones, 28
Alphonse, Efrain, 30, 37, 38, 108, 109
Amazon, 36
American Bible Society, 104, 113
Amos, 20
"anchor," 46
"angels ministered," 35
"anger," 127
Anglicans, 93
Anglo-Egyptian Sudan, 18, 30, 51, 109, 137, 140, 159, 168
Angola, 137, 172
Arabia, 76
Arabs, 13
archiereus, 79, 80
Areas of meaning, 61
Ariaga, Modesto, 113
Asian style in Greek, 69
"astonishment," 157
Augustine, 78
"authority," 19

Bali, 114, 115
"baptism of repentance," 33
Bazan, Enrique, 173
"believe," 21, 118-22
Bible
    authenticity, 66

communists' attitude toward, 169
culture, 35
distribution of, 165-177
geography, 35, 36
opposition to distribution, 174
some attitudes toward, 167-68
translation and publication, 14, 94, 95, 168, 172, 175
translators, 14, 15, 36, 37, 56, 61, 69, 70, 107, 117
Bingham, Hiram, 105-6
Bingham, Hiram, Jr., 105-6
"birthday," 44
Bishop of London, 90
Bishops' Bible, 92
"blessed," 43
Blind, Scriptures for, 175, 176
Bohemia, 83, 85, 86
Bolivia, 51, 111, 130, 151, 173, 176
Bonaparte, Prince Louis Lucien, 14
Borrowed words, 48, 49
"bowels," 39
Braille, 176
"breath," 44
British and Foreign Bible Society, 101, 103
"Brother Sherry," 103-5
Buddhism, 23
Buddhist, 26
Burma, 22, 95, 96
Burmese Bible, 97
"burned him up," 50

Camargo, Candelaria, 115
Canadian Baptist Mission, 113

Mistakes
  cultural analysis, 47
  in translating, 43-49
  in understanding, 30
Mizpah declaration, 18
Mohammedans, 26
Mongolian Dictionary, 105
Monmouth, Sir Humphrey, 91
Morrison, Robert, 97-99, 168
Mossi, 46, 51, 119, 128, 130, 133, 134, 150
Mozambique, 117
muguwump, 94
"my day," 17
Myers, Estella, 20
Mythological beliefs, 51

Negative expression, 32
nephesh, 65
Nestorian Christians, 76
Nesutan, Job, 94
Netherlands Bible Society, 114, 172
"new birth," 50
New Testament
  background for translating, 57
  grammatical style, 75
  languages into which translated, 14
  literary style, 23
  quotations from Old Testament, 69
ngobö, 38
Nicaragua, 51, 126, 129, 132
Nilotic language, 30
Nommensen, 171

"obey," 21, 121
"of," 32
"offend," 152-53
Old Testament, 80
  quotations in the New Testament, 69
Old usages, challenging of, 18
orthography, intricacies of, 22
Oruro, 173, 176

Palestine, 80
Panama, 19, 44, 50, 108, 120, 130
Paraclete, 20, 163
Parallels, cultural, 37-39
Parts of speech, differences between languages, 33
"patience," 130
Paul, style of, 70, 111
"peace," 40, 128-30
Peasants' War, 88
Pentecost, the miracle of, 74
"perhaps," 49
Persecutions, of Waldensians, 83-84
Persia, 76, 103
Persson, J. A., 117
"persuasion," 157-58
Peru, 35, 46, 111, 121, 123, 151, 159, 160, 161
Peshito, 76
philê, 126
phileô, 63
Philippines, 49, 164
Plevna, 77
Poland, 83
Poor Priests, 85
Port Said, 175
"prayer," 42, 158
"preaching upon the house tops," 57
"prevent," 58
Price, Jonathan, 96
"pride," 151
Pronunciation of strange sounds, 28-32
"prophet," 20
purísima, 48
Puritans, 93
Purvey, John, 85

Quiroga, Vicente, 166

"reconciliation," 140-41
Red Sea, 175
"redeem," 13
"redeemer," 159